5TH BIBLE READING MARATHON
A 26-WEEK TOPICAL BIBLE READING SCHEDULE

ask for the Old Paths
BIBLE QUESTIONS ANSWERED

Thus says the LORD, Stand you in the ways, and see, and ask for the old paths, where the good way is, and walk in it, and you shall find rest for your souls. (Jeremiah 6:16 NKJV)

Bible Reading Schedule Contributors

HOMER ANDERSON (1)	RUTH HARRISON (2)	JOHN MANFRA (25)
MYRA ANDERSON (5)	KENNY HOLTON (3)	DEBBIE & MIKE PAINE (18)
KEVIN BOYD (13)	G. R. HOLTON (21,24)	CARRIE SEAT (20)
BYRON BROWN (7)	JOHN HUNT (9)	DON SEAT (12)
JANET BROWN (8)	MARILYN & JOHN KING (15)	TONI WEBB (23)
CHERYL & DONNY BRYAN(6)	JOHN KLIMKO (26)	MARIE WEEKS (4)
FRANCINE COPPAGE (17)	AL LITTLE & BILL BROCK(19)	LEON WEEKS (11)
JERRY DELOACH (10)	DON LOCKEY (16)	
RICHARD HAMLEN (14)	BILL MALONE (22)	

The BIBLE READING MARATHON was developed to encourage regular reading of the Bible, the inspired inerrant Word of God. Developing this habit will build your faith in God, stimulate your spiritual growth, and answer your important questions of life.

SPONSORED AND DEVELOPED BY THE CENTRAL AVENUE CHURCH OF CHRIST

304 EAST CENTRAL AVENUE - VALDOSTA, GEORGIA

PHONE: (229) 242-6115 <central@cacoc.com>

5th BIBLE READING MARATHON

"ask...for the Old Paths"
BIBLE QUESTIONS ANSWERED
A 26-WEEK TOPICAL BIBLE READING SCHEDULE

Editor

G. R. Holton

Copy Reviewers

Debbie Paine

Marie Weeks

Kevin Boyd

Cover Photo

John Klimko

Growing Panes Articles

G. R. Holton

Published by

GROWING PANES, INC.
3543 Raintree Drive
Valdosta, Georgia 31601

Contact: grholton@yahoo.com

ISBN: 978-0-9905499-5-6

ISBN: 0-9905499-5-X

Copyright © 2016 Gresham R. Holton, Ph.D.

ALL RIGHTS RESERVED

Printed by CreateSpace, An Amazon.com Company

Available from Amazon.com, CreateSpace.com, Growing Panes, Inc.,
and other retail outlets

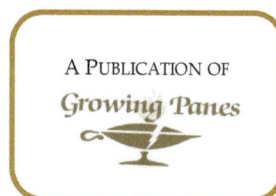

A PUBLICATION OF
Growing Panes

Contents Reading Schedule

A Matter of Heart and Habit

Jesus said, *"Blessed are the pure in heart, for they shall see God."*

Jesus is concerned about our heart! The heart is what you are, in the secrecy of your thought and feeling, when nobody knows but God. And what you are at the invisible root matters as much to God as what you are at the visible branch. "Man looks on the outward appearance, but the God looks on the heart" (1 Samuel 16:7). All the issues of life come from the heart.

> What comes out of the mouth proceeds from the heart . . . For out of the heart come evil thoughts, murder, adultery, fornication, theft, false witness, slander. These are what defile a man. (Matthew 15:18–19)

> Either make the tree good, and its fruit good; or make the tree bad, and its fruit bad; for the tree is known by its fruit . . . For out of the abundance of the heart the mouth speaks. (Matthew 12:33–34)

> A good man out of the good treasure of his heart brings forth good; and an evil man out of the evil treasure of his heart brings forth evil. For out of the abundance of the heart his mouth speaks. (Luke 6:45)

So the nature and condition of our heart is utterly crucial to Jesus. What we are in the deep, private recesses of our lives is what he cares about most. Jesus did not come into the world simply because we have some bad habits that need to be broken. He came into the world because we have dirty hearts that need to be purified. *How do we purify our hearts?*

David in Psalms 51:10 gives us the answer, "Create in me a clean heart, O God, And renew a steadfast spirit within me." Psalm 119:9 says, "How can a young man cleanse his way (keep his way pure)? By taking heed according to Your word." In Ephesians 5:26 the Apostle Paul tells us that God plans to make His church holy by the washing with water through the word. *Taking heed to God's word is the process that makes you pure and holy.*

The Bible Reading Marathon (BRM) is just a tool to help you develop the habit of regularly reading the Bible! Not only will it produce a stronger faith, but you will learn how to become *pure and holy.* Constant contact with God through His Word will help you cleanse your heart and your life. Make it a habit!

A. *The Cue,* or trigger that begins the habit-forming cycle. The Marathon schedule includes posted scriptures, a timetable for reading, and beginning and end cues.

B. *The Routine,* or the behavior patterns that must become repetitive over time. On a regular (or daily) basis, you will repeat the same behavior, i. e., complete the Bible reading schedule.

C. *The Rewards,* or the positive, good feeling you experience for completing the behavior and completing the course.

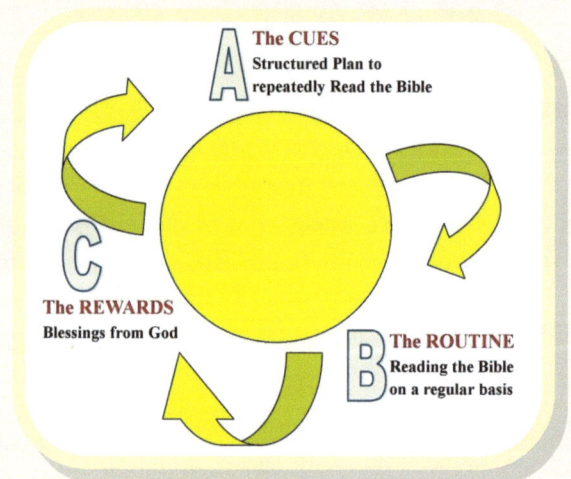

A The CUES
Structured Plan to repeatedly Read the Bible

C The REWARDS
Blessings from God

B The ROUTINE
Reading the Bible on a regular basis

Habit Cycle chart adapted from Charles Duhigg, *The Power of Habit*

The theme of our 5th Bible Reading Marathon is "'ask . . . for the Old Paths' - BIBLE QUESTIONS ANSWERED." All the readings this year will focus on actual questions taken directly from the Bible, such as one of the most important questions, *"Sirs, what must I do to be saved?"* (Acts 16:30). The BRM series is a topical reading schedule. Each of the weekly schedules has been re-searched and developed by serious Bible students, mostly by experienced adult class teachers. Below is the list of the topical series we have read (or will read) together:

BRM No. 1 - Read the Bible Through (2012)

BRM No. 2 - These Things We Believe (2013)

BRM No. 3 - Standing on the Promises of God (2014)

BRM No. 4 - Our God...an Awesome God! (2015)

BRM No. 5 - "ask... for the Old Paths" (2016)

The prophet Jeremiah pleaded with his people to return to God:

Thus said the LORD, Stand you in the ways, and see, and ask for the old paths, where is the good way, and walk therein, and you shall find rest for your souls. But they said, We will not walk therein. (Jeremiah 6:16 NKJV)

The people of God forgot Him and went further and further away from Him:

For My people have forgotten Me, They burn incense to worthless gods And they have stumbled from their ways, From the ancient paths, To walk in bypaths, Not on a highway...(Jeremiah 18:15).

Will you steal, murder, and commit adultery and swear falsely, and offer sacri-fices to Baal and walk after other gods that you have not known (Jeremiah 7:9).

In many ways our world is no different. It is easy to forget God amidst the glitter of work, fun and even religion. We are a busy people! Too busy! If we can't find time to listen to the voice of God through the words of the Bible, then *we are too busy*!

That's what the BRM is all about! It is a scheduled plan to help us get back to God if we have forgotten Him. But, it is also a daily exercise to help us maintain our connection to Him. In addi-tion, reading the Bible will just make us better people! God's Word truly is a "lamp" that lights our paths. The Bible says:

This is the message we have heard from him and declare to you: God is light; in him there is no darkness at all. If we claim to have fellowship with him and yet walk in the darkness, we lie and do not live out the truth. But if we walk in the light, as he is in the light, we have fellowship with one another, and the blood of Jesus, his Son, purifies us from all sin (1 John 1:5-7 NKJV).

May God bless you in answering many of your questions!

The Marathon is designed for both the young or beginning Bible reading "runners" and the more mature experienced Bible students.

- The *INSIDE TRACK* is for those who choose to read short passages of Scripture.

- The *MIDDLE LANES* schedule readings that summarize the topic of the week with narratives and longer passages of Scripture. Most runners will exercise in the *MIDDLE LANES*.

- For those who are really serious about developing a regular habit of Bible reading, the *FAST TRACK* requires the most time and discipline. If you take the *FAST TRACK* you will read all the Scriptures in the *INSIDE LANE*, the *MIDDLE LANES* and the *FAST TRACK*!

(Note: Some of the days have blank (_____) notations. You may add additional readings that you think apply to the question of the week. The idea of the BRM is to help us develop the habit of reading the Word of God for answers. The passages provided help, but the best source is your own research! Fill in the blanks with additional passages.)

Make the Commitment!

I want to join others in this spiritual exercise by entering this 26-week BIBLE READING MARATHON. I do hereby make the personal commitment to read my Bible regularly! I will dedicate a time each day to read the daily schedule. If I get behind, I will make every effort to catch up. I understand that I may re-enter the reading race at any time during the 26 weeks.

_____

(signed)

Command and teach these things. Don't let anyone look down on you because you are young, but set an example for the believers in speech, in conduct, in love, in faith and in purity. Until I come, devote yourself to the public reading of Scripture, to preaching and to teaching. Do not neglect your gift, which was given you through prophecy when the body of elders laid their hands on you.

Be diligent in these matters; give yourself wholly to them, so that everyone may see your progress. Watch your life and doctrine closely. Persevere in them, because if you do, you will save both yourself and your hearers. (1 Timothy 4:11-16 NIV)

COMMITMENT   Be Diligent!

"All Scripture Is Inspired by God"

KERRY HOLTON
ENCOURAGING YOUR PURSUIT OF GOD

I sincerely believe that the Bible is the book to which people must go for settling life's momentous questions. I believe it shows us how to become disciples of Jesus and how to live the Christian life. I believe it explains how it is that we can have a relationship with God and draw closer to him. But, why do I place such a high value on scripture? Why do I believe in the authority of the Bible?

I regard the Bible to be authoritative in my life. I am convinced that 2 Timothy 3:16 is true. You may remember that this passage from the New Testament makes the claim that *"all scripture is God-breathed."* My firm conviction is that there was a supernatural influence upon the writers of the biblical texts. Granted, however, that just because the Bible claims to be inspired does not make it so. I want to give you my rationale for believing the Bible. *Here is one of many reasons I believe in biblical inspiration.*

Let's begin by examining how Jesus himself regarded scripture. You may not be surprised to learn that **Jesus had a high view of scripture.** For example, he quoted a statement found in Genesis 2:24 and attributed that statement to God (Matthew 19:5). He quoted a statement found in Psalm 110 and declared that David made that declaration "by the Holy Spirit" (Mark 12:36). He referred to Psalm 82 and emphatically stated that *"scripture cannot be broken"* (John 10:35).

Jesus appealed to what was written in the Old Testament to substantiate his own claims. (See, for example, Luke 4:16-21; Mark 12:10; Luke 24:44,45; John 5:39-47.)

Furthermore, the manner in which he handled the temptation experience in the desert is a remarkable attestation to his belief in the authority of scripture. He answered every temptation with an *"It is written,"* followed by a quotation from the Old Testament (Matthew 4:4, 6, 7).

He answered questions from the religious leaders of his day by referring to what was written in the Old Testament. When asked what should be done to inherit eternal life, he replied: *"What is written in the law?"* (Luke 10:25-28). When criticized for allowing his disciples to pluck grain on the Sabbath, Jesus answered: *"Have you not read . . . ?"* and then, he referred to a story recorded in 1 Samuel 21. In fact, *"Have you not read,"* was one of our Lord's common responses to questions that challenged his behavior (Matthew 19:3-6; 12:23-32).

You ask: "Kerry, what are you trying to say with all of these New Testament references?" Just this: **Jesus believed in the authority of scripture.** We might well ask, "Why?" Why did Jesus have such a high view of scripture?

I'll tell you what I believe is the most reasonable answer to that question: *Jesus regarded the Old Testament writings to be inspired.* That is, again, he believed that *those writings were influenced by God.* I find proof of this in John 10:35 where Jesus referred to a statement in Psalm 82:6 as the "word of God." I find it in his reference to the fifth commandment of the Decalogue—honor your father and mother—as *"the commandment of God"* and *"the word of God"* (Mark 7:9-13). And I find it in the time when the Sadducees asked a question about marriage in the after-life, and Jesus quoted Exodus 3:6, referring to it as *"what was said to you by God."* These are just a few of the New Testament references that seem to show our Lord's belief that God's voice could be heard in the pages of the Old Testament.

Now, may I sum it up? **Why do I believe in the inspiration of scripture? Because I believe that Jesus believed in it.** Of course, this is enough for me, since the heart and soul of my faith is Jesus and what he believed, taught, and practiced.

-Adapted from "Connect3Ministries" website by Kerry Holton. "Like" Kerry on Facebook to receive weekly blogs and daily prayers.

THIS WEEK'S QUESTION:

OUR WORLD: *"Where were you when I laid the earth's foundation? Tell me, if you understand."* (Job 38:4)

WEEK 1

DATES

_____ TO _____

INSIDE TRACK   MIDDLE LANES   FAST TRACK

God the Creator: Planner, Creator, Sustainer

Earth's Foundation: Laws, Order, Design

Early Beginnings: Man, Woman, Animals

Man's Sinful World: Fall of Man, Corruption

What this Means to us Today

INSIDE TRACK	MIDDLE LANES	FAST TRACK
Monday:	**Monday:**	**Monday:**
☐ Isaiah 40:25-26	☐ Psalm 104:24-30	☐ Job 38:1-41
	☐ Job 26:5-14	☐ Psalm 19:7-9
	☐ Jeremiah 5:20-24	☐ Isaiah 51:12-15
		☐ Psalm 145:8-16
		☐ 1 Chronicles 16:23-34
Tuesday:	**Tuesday:**	**Tuesday:**
☐ Genesis 1:1	☐ Genesis 1:1-19	☐ Psalm 19:1-6
	☐ Genesis 2:1-14	☐ Psalm 104:1-9
	☐ Isaiah 40:12-14	☐ Proverb 8:22-31
		☐ Psalm 33:6-9
		☐ Psalm 148:1-6
Wednesday:	**Wednesday:**	**Wednesday:**
☐ Genesis 2:23-24	☐ Genesis 1:20-31	☐ Job 39:1-30
	☐ Genesis 2:15-25	☐ Job 40:15-24
	☐ Job 38:39-41	☐ Job 41:1-34
		☐ Psalm 104:10-23
		☐ Psalm 148:7-14
Thursday:	**Thursday:**	**Thursday:**
☐ Genesis 8:21	☐ Genesis 3:1-24	☐ Isaiah 59:1-20
	☐ Genesis 6:5-6	☐ Psalm 14:1-6
	☐ Proverb 6:16-19	☐ Isaiah 40:21-24
		☐ Matthew 15:18-20
		☐ Romans 1:18-32
Friday:	**Friday:**	**Friday:**
☐ Acts 17:29-30	☐ John 1:1-5	☐ Acts 17:22-31
	☐ Psalm 104:31-35	☐ Psalm 102:24-28
	☐ Isaiah 40:28-31	☐ Psalm 103:13-19
		☐ Psalm 106:1-2
		☐ _____

The fascinating story of how we got the Bible in its present form actually starts thousands of years ago. The original New Testament books were written in the Greek language, and the Old Testament books were written in Hebrew.

The first hand-written English language Bible manuscripts were produced in the 1380's AD by the "Morning Star of the Reformation" John Wycliffe, an Oxford professor, scholar, and theologian. Wycliffe was well-known throughout Europe for his opposition to the teaching of the organized Church, which he believed to be contrary to the Bible. Wycliffe, with the help of others, produced dozens of English language manuscript copies of the scriptures. They were translated out of the Latin Vulgate, which was the only source text available to Wycliffe. The Pope was so infuriated by his teachings and the Wycliffe translation of the Bible into English, that 44 years after Wycliffe had died, he ordered the bones to be dug-up, crushed, and scattered in the river!

IN the bigynnyng was the word, and the word was at God, and God was the word. This was in the biginnyng at God. Alle thingis weren maad by hym, and withouten him was maad no thing, that thing that was maad. In him was lyf, and the lyf was the

Growing Panes
No. 501

THIS WEEK'S QUESTION:

SIN'S CURSE: *"What is this that you have done?"*

Gen. 3:13 ESV

INSIDE TRACK | **MIDDLE LANES** | **FAST TRACK**

Causes of Sin

Monday:
- 1 John 3:8

Consequences of Sin

Tuesday:
- John 5:28-29

Examples of Sin

Wednesday:
- John 8:44

Penalty for Sin

Thursday:
- Exodus 34:6-7

What this Means to us Today

Friday:
- Romans 6:12

MIDDLE LANES

Monday:
- Genesis 3:1-13
- Joshua 7:10-21
- Luke 12:13-31

Tuesday:
- 2 Kings 17:7-20
- 2 Peter 2:1-12
- Jude vss.5-7

Wednesday:
- Jeremiah 7:9-15
- Acts 5:1-11
- Acts 8:14-23

Thursday:
- Numbers 14:20-35
- 1 Corinthians 5:1-11
- 1 Timothy 1:18-20

Friday:
- Luke 4:1-13
- Ephesians 5:3-7
- Haggai 1:3-11

FAST TRACK

Monday:
- John 8:42-47
- Romans 6:15-23
- James 1:19-27
- 1 Corinthians 10:6-13
- Ephesians 4:25-32

Tuesday:
- Jeremiah 11:6-14
- Numbers 12:1-12
- Hebrews 10:26-31
- 2 Thessalonians 1:5-10
- Matthew 27:3-5

Wednesday:
- 1 Kings 11:1-13
- Jeremiah 43:1-7
- Jeremiah 44:1-6
- Romans 3:9-20
- _____

Thursday:
- Numbers 20:9-13
- Nehemiah 9:26-27
- Psalm 106:24-33
- Romans 2:1-11
- _____

Friday:
- Ephesians 5:8-20
- Hebrews 5:8-14
- Hebrews 12:14-17
- James 4:1-10
- _____

One of Wycliffe's followers, John Hus, actively promoted Wycliffe's ideas: that people should be permitted to read the Bible in their own language, and they should oppose the tyranny of the Roman church that threatened anyone possessing a non-Latin Bible with execution. Hus was burned at the stake in 1415, with Wycliffe's manuscript Bibles used as kindling for the fire. The last words of John Hus were that, "*in 100 years, God will raise up a man whose calls for reform cannot be suppressed.*" Later, the reformer Martin Luther (1517) went on to

Latin Vulgate
1 John 3:8 qui facit peccatum ex diabolo est quoniam ab initio diabolus peccat in hoc apparuit Filius Dei ut dissolvat opera diaboli

be the first person to translate and publish the Bible in the commonly-spoken dialect of the German people. Foxe's Book of Martyrs records that in that same year, 1517, seven people were burned at the stake by the Roman Catholic Church for the crime of teaching their children to say the Lord's Prayer in English rather than Latin. Even up to the present time Latin is the official language used in the worship sacraments of the Roman Catholic Church.

Growing Panes
No. 502

WEEK 3

DATES

_____ TO _____

THIS WEEK'S QUESTION:

MAN'S NEED: *". . .what are mere mortals that you should think about them, human beings that you should care for them?"* - *Psalm 8:3-4 NLT*

INSIDE TRACK

In the Image of God

Monday:
- [ ] Genesis 1:26-27

Marred by Sin

Tuesday:
- [ ] Isaiah 53:6

Mortal but Eternal

Wednesday:
- [ ] Ecclesiastes 12:7

Insignificant but Dignified

Thursday:
- [ ] Psalm 103:11

What this Means to us Today

Friday:
- [ ] Hebrews 3:1

MIDDLE LANES

Monday:
- [ ] Genesis 2:4-7
- [ ] Genesis 5:1-3
- [ ] Genesis 9:1-6

Tuesday:
- [ ] Genesis 3:17-19
- [ ] Genesis 6:1-7
- [ ] Romans 3:9-18

Wednesday:
- [ ] John 11:17-27
- [ ] 2 Corinthians 5:1-10
- [ ] John 5:24-29

Thursday:
- [ ] Job 10:8-12
- [ ] Psalm 8:1-9
- [ ] 1 John 3:1-3

Friday:
- [ ] 2 Peter 1:3-4
- [ ] Matthew 5:13-16
- [ ] 2 Corinthians 5:16-21

FAST TRACK

Monday:
- [ ] Acts 17:22-29
- [ ] 1 Corinthians 11:3-9
- [ ] Hebrews 4:12-13
- [ ] 1 Thessalonians 5:23-24
- [ ] James 3:9-12

Tuesday:
- [ ] Romans 1:18-32
- [ ] Romans 5:12-21
- [ ] Galatians 5:19-21
- [ ] James 1:13-15
- [ ] Psalm 51:1-12

Wednesday:
- [ ] Luke 23:32-43
- [ ] 1 Corinthians 15:35-58
- [ ] 1 Thessalonians 4:13-18
- [ ] 2 Timothy 1:8-10
- [ ] Romans 8:18-25

Thursday:
- [ ] Isaiah 40:25-31
- [ ] Hebrews 1:5-18
- [ ] Romans 8:28-39
- [ ] Ephesians 2:1-10
- [ ] 1 Peter 2:4-10

Friday:
- [ ] Colossians 3:1-10
- [ ] 2 Corinthians 3:7-18
- [ ] Ephesians 4:17-24
- [ ] 1 Peter 4:1-11
- [ ] James 3:3-12

Johann Gutenberg invented the printing press in the 1450's, in Mainz, Germany. Gutenberg's Latin Bibles were beautiful with colorfully hand-illuminated pages. Obviously, the invention of the printing press had a major impact on reading the Bible. However, Gutenberg died in poverty after his business partners took control of his business. The invention of the printing press meant that Bibles and books could finally be effectively produced in large quantities in a short period of time. In the 1490's the personal physician to King Henry the 7th and 8th, Thomas Linacre, decided to learn Greek. After reading the Gospels in Greek, and comparing it to the Latin Vulgate, he wrote in his diary, "Either this (the original Greek) is not the Gospel... or we are not Christians." The Church threatened to kill anyone who read the scripture in any language other than Latin; even though the New Testament was originally written in Greek and the Old Testament in Hebrew. Today, the most common language of the world is English. Thus, the development of the English translations is important.

> **Hebrews 3:1** Greek
> οθεν αδελφοι αγιοι κλησεως επουρανιου μετ οχοι κατανοησατε τον αποστολον και αρχι ερεα της ομολογιας ημων ιησουν

Growing Panes

No. 503

WORLDLINESS: *"What good will it be for someone to gain the whole world, yet forfeit their soul? Or what can anyone give in exchange for their soul?"* - Matthew 16:26 NIV

WEEK 4

DATES
_____ TO _____

Topics	INSIDE TRACK	MIDDLE LANES	FAST TRACK
Lust of the Flesh	**Monday:** ☐ Romans 8:5	**Monday:** ☐ Romans 8:6-14 ☐ Galatians 5:13-26 ☐ Romans 1:26-32	**Monday:** ☐ Ephesians 2:1-5 ☐ Romans 13:11-14 ☐ Galatians 6:7-8 ☐ Jeremiah 17:9-10 ☐ Romans 7:14-20
Lust of the Eyes	**Tuesday:** ☐ Proverb 23:5	**Tuesday:** ☐ Matthew 4:1-11 ☐ 2 Samuel 11:1-26 ☐ Exodus 20:1-17	**Tuesday:** ☐ Matthew 5:27-30 ☐ Proverb 6:20-29 ☐ Numbers 15:37-41 ☐ Mark 10:17-22 ☐ Habakkuk 1:13
Pride of Life	**Wednesday:** ☐ Romans 12:3	**Wednesday:** ☐ Isaiah 2:6-18 ☐ Psalm 10:2-11 ☐ Isaiah 9:8-17	**Wednesday:** ☐ Psalm 59:10-13 ☐ Revelation 3:14-22 ☐ Ezekiel 28:4-5 ☐ Ezekiel 28:17-19 ☐ Proverb 21:2-4
Examples of Worldliness	**Thursday:** ☐ Genesis 3:6	**Thursday:** ☐ 1 Samuel 15:12-23 ☐ Exodus 32:1-6 ☐ Acts 5:1-11	**Thursday:** ☐ Judges 14:1-3 ☐ Genesis 13:8-13 ☐ Ezekiel 16:49-50 ☐ Ephesians 4:17-19 ☐ 2 Peter 2:4-12
What this Means to us Today	**Friday:** ☐ 1 John 2:15-17	**Friday:** ☐ 1 Corinthians 10:1-13 ☐ Philippians 3:12-21 ☐ Deuteronomy 8:1-20	**Friday:** ☐ Matthew 16:24-27 ☐ Hebrews 4:12-16 ☐ James 4:4-7 ☐ 1 John 5:18-19 ☐ Romans 12:1-2

Romans 8:5 King James Bible
For they that are after the flesh do mind the things of the flesh; but they that are after the Spirit the things of the Spirit.

In 1496, John Colet, the son of the Mayor of London, started reading the New Testament in Greek and translating it into English for the public at Saint Paul's Cathedral in London. The people were so hungry to hear the Word of God in a language they could understand, that within six months there were 20,000 people packed in the church. The great scholar Erasmus (1469-1536) was so moved by Colet's desire to correct the corrupt Latin Vulgate, that in 1516 he published a Greek-Latin Parallel New Testament. This was the first non-Latin Vulgate text of the scripture to be produced in a millennium... and the first ever to come off a printing press. The Greek-Latin New Testament of Erasmus focused on correcting the corrupt Latin Vulgate by comparing the original Greek (New Testament) with the Latin Vulgate. No sympathy for this "illegal activity" was to be found from Rome. This text was used by Martin Luther and Tyndale for their translations and later by translators of the Geneva Bible and the King James Version. Leo X declared "the fable of Christ was quite profitable to him."

Growing Panes

No. 504

THIS WEEK'S QUESTION:

PERSONAL PURITY: "How can a young person keep his life pure? [He can do it] by holding on to your word."
-Psalm 119:9 God's Word Translation

	INSIDE TRACK	MIDDLE LANES	FAST TRACK
Purity Within	**Monday:** ☐ Matthew 5:8	**Monday:** ☐ John 1:43-51 ☐ John 14:6-11 ☐ Psalm 119:33-40	**Monday:** ☐ Leviticus 20:22-26 ☐ Matthew 15:1-20 ☐ Galatians 5:16-25 ☐ Psalm 51:6-12 ☐ Matthew 23:25-28
Securing the Heart	**Tuesday:** ☐ Psalm 19:14	**Tuesday:** ☐ Psalm 24:3-6 ☐ Psalm 119:1-8 ☐ Romans 12:1-3	**Tuesday:** ☐ Proverb 4:20-27 ☐ 1 Peter 1:13-25 ☐ Psalm 119:9-16 ☐ Psalm 19:7-14 ☐ _____
Sins of Youth	**Wednesday:** ☐ Psalm 119:9	**Wednesday:** ☐ Ecclesiastes 11:9-10 ☐ Psalm 25:4-10 ☐ 2 Timothy 2:20-26	**Wednesday:** ☐ 1 Kings 12:1-20 ☐ Ecclesiastes 10:1-2 ☐ Isaiah 59:1-21 ☐ Romans 6:17-19 ☐ _____ **Thursday:** ☐ Genesis 39:1-23
Youth Examples	**Thursday:** ☐ Luke 2:51-52	**Thursday:** ☐ Matthew 18:1-6 ☐ 2 Timothy 3:14-15 ☐ Ecclesiastes 4:13-15	☐ Hebrews 11:24-26 ☐ 1 Kings 3:3-14 ☐ Daniel 1:3-21 ☐ Daniel 3:1-30 ☐
What this Means to us Today	**Friday:** ☐ Proverb 4:23	**Friday:** ☐ 1 John 1:5-10 ☐ Galatians 5:22-26 ☐ Jude 1:19-20	**Friday:** ☐ 1 Corinthians 6:9-11 ☐ 1 John 3:1-10 ☐ Galatians 6:7-10 ☐ Romans 12:9-21 ☐ Revelation 2:8-11 ☐

William Tyndale holds the distinction of being the first man to ever print the New Testament in the English language. He was so fluent in eight languages that it was said no one would think any one of them to be his native tongue. With the Erasmus translation as a source, Tyndale showed up on Martin Luther's doorstep in Germany in 1525, and by year's end had translated the New Testament into English. He had been forced to flee England, because of the widespread rumor that the Tyndale English New Testament project was underway, causing inquisitors and bounty hunters to be con-

> **Matthew 5:8**
> Blessed are the pure in herte: for they shall se God. Tyndale Translation

stantly on Tyndale's trail to arrest him and prevent his project. In 1525-1526 the Tyndale New Testament became the first printed edition of the scripture in the English language. One risked death by burning if caught in mere possession of Tyndale's forbidden books. They were burned as soon as the Bishop could confiscate them, but copies trickled through and actually ended up in the bedroom of King Henry VIII. Books and Bibles flowed into England in bales of cotton and sacks of flour. The people craved copies to read!

Growing Panes

No. 505

THIS WEEK'S QUESTION:

MISSION: *"Whom shall I send? And who will go for us?"*

-Isaiah 6:8 KJV

INSIDE TRACK / MIDDLE LANES / FAST TRACK

Topic	INSIDE TRACK	MIDDLE LANES	FAST TRACK
Mission of John the Baptizer	**Monday:** ☐ Luke 1:13-17	**Monday:** ☐ Matthew 3:1-3 ☐ Mark 1:1-11 ☐ Luke 1:5-25	**Monday:** ☐ Luke 1:57-80 ☐ Luke 3:1-22 ☐ John 1:16-18 ☐ Matthew 26:26-30 ☐ _____
Mission to the Jews Only	**Tuesday:** ☐ Exodus 34:10	**Tuesday:** ☐ Exodus 34:11-14 ☐ Exodus 20:1-16 ☐ _____	**Tuesday:** ☐ Exodus 34:15-27 ☐ Matthew 11:20-24 ☐ Luke 10:1-20 ☐ Luke 10:25-40 ☐ _____
Mission to the Entire World	**Wednesday:** ☐ Matthew 28:19-20	**Wednesday:** ☐ Luke 9:23-27 ☐ Mark 16:14-20 ☐ Matthew 28:16-20	**Wednesday:** ☐ Acts 6:1-7 ☐ 2 Corinthians 4:1-18 ☐ 2 Corinthians 5:1-21 ☐ Mark 4:14-20 ☐ _____
Mission of the Lord's Church	**Thursday:** ☐ Romans 1:16-17	**Thursday:** ☐ Acts 1:12-26 ☐ Acts 2:37-47 ☐ Acts 4:19-36	**Thursday:** ☐ Acts 3:17-26 ☐ Acts 14:21-23 ☐ Hebrews 9:26-28 ☐ _____ ☐ _____
What this Means to us Today	**Friday:** ☐ Ephesians 5:15-16	**Friday:** ☐ Romans 14:12 ☐ Ephesians 4:17-31 ☐ 1 Corinthians 14:40	**Friday:** ☐ 1 Corinthians 14:26-40 ☐ 1 Corinthians 16:1-4 ☐ 1 Corinthians 1:10-13 ☐ Hebrew 10:25-29 ☐ Matthew 26:26-30

Today, there are only two known copies left of Tyndale's 1525-26 First Edition. Ironically, Tyndale's biggest customer was the King's men, who would buy up every copy available to burn them... and Tyndale used their money to print even more! In the end, Tyndale was caught and incarcerated for 500 days before he was strangled and burned at the stake in 1536. Tyndale's last words were, *"Oh Lord, open the King of England's eyes".* Myles Coverdale and John "Thomas Matthew" Rogers had remained loyal disciples the last six years of Tyndale's

Romans 14:12 Therefore each of us shall yield reason to God for himself. (And so each of us shall have to answer, or to give an account, for himself, to God.) Wycliffe Bible

life, and they carried the English Bible project forward and even accelerated it. Coverdale finished translating and printing the first complete (Old and New Testaments) English Bible on October 4, 1535. It is known as the Coverdale Bible. Tyndale's prayer would be answered just three years after his death in 1539, when King Henry VIII finally allowed, and even funded, the printing of an English Bible known as the "Great Bible".

Growing Panes No. 506

God gives the directions!

Just imagine you have a very important appointment in a faraway place that is hundreds of miles away. You are neither familiar with the location of the appointment, nor have you traveled that way before. A few miles out you stop to ask for directions. You are not even sure you are even going in the right direction. The answers you get on "how to get there" are confusing, and you begin to realize that you are lost! Finally, you stop at a gas station to ask for directions. Like the others, the attendant has a vague idea of where you are going, but he does give you a roadmap with explicit directions.

What does this have to do with reading the Bible? Very simple. The Bible is a spiritual "roadmap" directing us toward our final destination, heaven...or hell!

The miracle of the ages is that our God speaks to us and tells us how to live and what to expect when this life is over. God has given us directions for our twenty-first century journey of life. He has supplied us with this spiritual roadmap, the Bible, which answers our questions about the direction we are going. And, contrary to what you may think, the directions are clear and understandable!

God, who at sundry times and in divers manners spake in time past unto the fathers by the prophets, Hath in these last days spoken unto us by his Son, whom he hath appointed heir of all things, by whom also he made the worlds; Who being the brightness of his glory, and the express image of his person, and upholding all things by the word of his power, when he had by himself purged our sins, sat down on the right hand of the Majesty on high (Hebrews 1:1-3).

Directions are important as we journey. What would happen if we had no traffic laws? Or traffic lights? Or signs beside the road? Taking the journey is enjoyable, but the real reward is when we get there! We all have asked the simple question, "Are we there yet?" Our "spiritual" roadmap answers that: "No" for we have all sinned (Romans 3:23) but as we draw closer to God we come to know Him better and love Him more. Our Bible says "If you love me, you will obey what I command" (John 14:15).

Clear instructions are given to us on "How" we should live our lives. For example, we are told to "love one another" (John 13:34-35) and to "deny ourselves" (Matthew 16:24). The Bible directs us to "help the poor and needy" (James 1:27) and to help others who have taken a wrong road in life (1 Thessalonians 5:6-8). Successful travelers "abide in Christ" (John 15:4,8) to make sure they go in the right direction. Another way of saying it is, "be doers of the word and not hearers only" (James 1:22-25).

So, it's not enough to just have a good roadmap, but you must trust in it and follow it.

Finally, the Bible reminds us of the most important appointment we have to make, which is to meet God in judgment:

And as it is appointed unto men once to die, but after this the judgment (Hebrews 9:27).

Where can we find reliable information? Are there directions to guide us confidently through the twenty-first century? There are. The Bible provides clear, understandable answers to the deepest questions of the human heart. More than five hundred such questions are found in the Bible. Many of these questions will be answered as you run this *BIBLE READING MARATHON*!

THIS WEEK'S QUESTION:

HIS CHURCH: "But what about you?" he asked.
"Who do you say I am?" - Matthew 16:15 NIV

INSIDE TRACK | MIDDLE LANES | FAST TRACK

Built on Jesus, God's Son

The Kingdom of God

Body of the Saved

God's Family, Saved to Serve

What this Means to us Today

INSIDE TRACK

Monday:
- [ ] Matthew 16:18

Tuesday:
- [ ] Daniel 2:44

Wednesday:
- [ ] 1 Corinthians 12:13

Thursday:
- [ ] Galatians 5:13

Friday:
- [ ] 1 Corinthians 1:10

MIDDLE LANES

Monday:
- [ ] 1 Corinthians 3:9-11
- [ ] Colossians 1:15-18
- [ ] Ephesians 2:19-22

Tuesday:
- [ ] Mark 1:14-15
- [ ] Mark 9:1-8
- [ ] Mark 10:13-26

Wednesday:
- [ ] Acts 2:42-47
- [ ] Ephesians 1:22-23
- [ ] Ephesians 4:1-16

Thursday:
- [ ] Matthew 6:24
- [ ] Matthew 20:25-28
- [ ] Matthew 25:14-30

Friday:
- [ ] 1 Corinthians 10:31-33
- [ ] Colossians 1:3-14
- [ ] Revelation 3:21-22

FAST TRACK

Monday:
- [ ] Matthew 16:13-20
- [ ] John 10:7-18
- [ ] 1 Peter 2:4-10
- [ ] Romans 15:17-20
- [ ] 1 Timothy 3:14-15

Tuesday:
- [ ] Luke 9:2-27
- [ ] Luke 17:20-21
- [ ] John 3:3-5
- [ ] Acts 28:30-31
- [ ] 1 Corinthians 15:22-28

Wednesday:
- [ ] Romans 12:1-7
- [ ] 1 Corinthians 12:12-31
- [ ] Ephesians 3:2-6
- [ ] Ephesians 5:23-30
- [ ] Colossians 1:24

Thursday:
- [ ] Matthew 25:31-46
- [ ] Mark 9:33-37
- [ ] Luke 22:24-26
- [ ] John 12:26
- [ ] Romans 12:3-8

Friday:
- [ ] Ephesians 3:10-21
- [ ] Ephesians 5:3-7
- [ ] Hebrews 12:22-25
- [ ] Revelation 22:12-17
- [ ] Colossians 3:23-25

> **Matthew 16:18** And I saye also unto the yt thou arte Peter: and apon this rocke I wyll bylde my congregacion. And the gates of hell shall not prevayle ageynst it.
> **Matthew-Tyndale Bible**

John Rogers went on to print the second complete English Bible in 1537. It was, however, the first English Bible translated from the original Biblical languages of Hebrew and Greek. He printed it under the pseudonym "Thomas Matthew," (an assumed name that had actually been used by Tyndale at one time) whose writings had been condemned by the English authorities. It is a composite made up of Tyndale's Pentateuch and New Testament (1534-1535 edition), Coverdale's Bible and some of Roger's own translation of the text. It remains known most commonly as the Matthew-Tyndale Bible.

It went through a nearly identical second-edition printing in 1549. In 1539, Thomas Cranmer, the Archbishop of Canterbury, hired Myles Coverdale at the bequest of King Henry VIII to publish the "Great Bible." It became the first English Bible authorized for public use. It was distributed to every church, and chained to the pulpit. A reader was even provided so that the illiterate could hear the Word of God in plain English. Cranmer's Bible, published by Coverdale, was known as the Great Bible due to its great size: a large pulpit folio measuring over 14 inches tall.

THIS WEEK'S QUESTION:

SALVATION: *"Sirs, what must I do to be saved?"*

- Acts 16:30 KJV

DATES
_____ TO _____

INSIDE TRACK

The Gospel of Christ
_____
_____
_____
_____
_____

Monday:
☐ Romans 1: 16, 17

Righteousness of God
_____
_____
_____
_____

Tuesday:
☐ Psalm 32:1, 2

Examples in Acts of Conversions
_____
_____
_____
_____
_____

Wednesday:
☐ Acts 6:7

Saved Now and for Eternity
_____
_____
_____
_____
_____

Thursday:
☐ Isaiah 12:2

What This Means Today
_____
_____
_____
_____
_____

Friday:
☐ Psalm 119:137, 138

MIDDLE LANES

Monday:
☐ Matthew 27:32-50
☐ Matthew 28:1-10
☐ Mark 16:15-16

Tuesday:
☐ Nehemiah 9:7, 8
☐ Psalm 89:14-18
☐ _____

Wednesday:
☐ Acts 2:36-48
☐ Acts 4:32-37
☐ Acts 11:19-24

Thursday:
☐ John 3:16-21
☐ Acts 16:29-34
☐ Ephesians 2:1-10

Friday:
☐ Ephesians 6:10-18
☐ 2 Peter 3:11-18
☐ 1 John 2:15-17

FAST TRACK

Monday:
☐ Luke 23:26-56
☐ Mark 16:1-8
☐ Matthew 28:18-20
☐ 1 Corinthians 15:3-8
☐

Tuesday:
☐ Isaiah 45:18-25
☐ Isaiah 51:7, 8
☐ Psalm 71:14-19
☐ Romans 3:21-26
☐ Philippians 3:7-11

Wednesday:
☐ Acts 8:9-13
☐ Acts 8:26-40
☐ Acts 9:1-19
☐ Acts 10:44-48
☐ Acts 16:11-15

Thursday:
☐ Psalm 27:1-14
☐ 1 Timothy 1:12-17
☐ 2 Timothy 1:8-12
☐ Titus 3:3-8
☐ 1 Peter 3:18-22

Friday:
☐ Mark 8:34-38
☐ John 19:14-42
☐ 2 Corinthians 10:3-5
☐ Titus 2:11-15
☐ Genesis 3:1-8

It was not that King Henry VIII had a change of conscience regarding publishing the Bible in English. His motives were more sinister. King Henry VIII had, in fact, requested that the Pope permit him to divorce his wife and marry his mistress. The Pope refused. King Henry responded by marrying his mistress anyway, (later having two of his many wives executed), and thumbing his nose at the Pope by renouncing Roman Catholicism. This new Church, neither Roman Catholic nor truly Protestant, became known as the Anglican Church or the Church of England. His first

> **Genesis 3:7** Then the eyes of them both were opened, and they knew that they were naked, and they sewed fig tree leaves together, and made themselves breeches. **The Geneva Bible**

act was to further defy the wishes of Rome by funding the printing of the scriptures in English... the first legal English Bible... just for spite.

Myles Coverdale led a group that included John Foxe, John Calvin and John Knox to produce a Bible to educate their families while they were in exile in Geneva, Switzerland. Generally known as the Geneva Bible, it also was called the "britches" bible because of how passages in Genesis were translated. The translators of the 1611 King James Bible were greatly influenced by the Geneva Bible.

Growing Panes
No. 508

THIS WEEK'S QUESTION:

BAPTISM: "*How can someone be born when they are old?*" ..."*Surely they cannot enter a second time into their mother's womb to be born!*" - John 3:4 NIV

WEEK 9

DATES
_____TO_____

INSIDE TRACK	MIDDLE LANES	FAST TRACK

Baptism: The New Birth

Purpose of Baptism

Faith and Baptism

Examples of Baptism in New Testament

What this Means to us Today

INSIDE TRACK

Monday:
- [ ] John 3:3

Tuesday:
- [ ] Acts 2:38-39

Wednesday:
- [ ] Mark 16:14-16

Thursday:
- [ ] Luke 3:21-22

Friday:
- [ ] Acts 22:16

MIDDLE LANES

Monday:
- [ ] John 3:1-8
- [ ] Colossians 2:11-15
- [ ] Titus 3:1-8

Tuesday:
- [ ] 1 Corinthians 12:12-20
- [ ] Ephesians 4:1-6
- [ ] 1 Peter 3:13-32

Wednesday:
- [ ] Luke 7:27-35
- [ ] Acts 22:6-16
- [ ] _____

Thursday:
- [ ] Matthew 3:13-17
- [ ] Acts 16:11-34
- [ ] Acts 18:5-11

Friday:
- [ ] John 1:6-18
- [ ] 2 Thess. 2:13-17
- [ ] 1 Timothy 2:1-7

FAST TRACK

Monday:
- [ ] Romans 6:1-14
- [ ] Ephesians 4:17-32
- [ ] Colossians 3:1-11
- [ ] 2 Corinthians 5:16-19
- [ ] Acts 11:16-18

Tuesday:
- [ ] Matthew 3:1-12
- [ ] Mark 1:1-8
- [ ] Luke 3:7-17
- [ ] Acts 19:1-10
- [ ] 1 Corinthians 1:10-17

Wednesday:
- [ ] Matthew 21:18-27
- [ ] Romans 10:5-10
- [ ] Galatians 3:19-20
- [ ] Hebrews 11:1-12
- [ ] 1 Corinthians 10:1-5

Thursday:
- [ ] Acts 2:36-42
- [ ] Acts 8:26-40
- [ ] Acts 9:10-19
- [ ] Acts 22:1-16
- [ ] Luke 3:1-6

Friday:
- [ ] Matthew 28:16-20
- [ ] Acts 4:1-12
- [ ] Colossians 3:12-17
- [ ] Titus 2:11-15
- [ ] _____

The Geneva Bible retained over 90% of William Tyndale's original English translation. The Geneva Bible was the one used by the Puritans and Pilgrims. It was the first Bible brought to America by the Puritans. In 1568, the Bishop's Bible , which was a revision of the Great Bible, was introduced. Despite nineteen editions being printed between 1568 and 1606, this Bible, referred to as the "rough draft of the King James Version," was never popular with the people. In 1582, the Church of Rome surrendered their fight for "Latin

Acts 2:38 But Peter said to them: Do penance, and be baptized every one of you in the name of Jesus Christ, for the remission of your sins: and you shall receive the gift of the Holy Ghost.
Douai-Rheims Translation

only" and decided that if the Bible was to be available in English, they would at least have an official Roman Catholic English translation commonly called the Douai-Rheims Version. Based on the corrupt and inaccurate Latin Vulgate as the only source text, this translation had all the distortions and corruptions revealed by Erasmus years earlier. Because it was translated at the Roman Catholic College in the city of Rheims, it was known as the Rheims New Testament (also spelled Rhemes). The Douay Old Testament was translated in the city of Douay (also spelled Doway and Douai).

Growing Panes

No. 509

THIS WEEK'S QUESTION:

HOLY TEACHING: *"Now a certain ruler asked him, "Good teacher, what must I do to inherit eternal life?"*
- Luke 18:18, NET Bible

INSIDE TRACK

Being an Example

Monday:
- [ ] 1 Corinthians 12:27

Teaching the Truth

Tuesday:
- [ ] Psalm 25:5-7

Teach to Observe all Things

Wednesday:
- [ ] Matthew 28:18-20

Hearer's Responsibilities

Thursday:
- [ ] John 14:15

What this Means to us Today

Friday:
- [ ] John 16:13-15

MIDDLE LANES

Monday:
- [ ] 1 Timothy 4:12
- [ ] Titus 2:3
- [ ] Titus 2:7

Tuesday:
- [ ] John 17:17-19
- [ ] John 8:31-32
- [ ] James 1:22-25

Wednesday:
- [ ] Colossians 3:23-24
- [ ] Deuteronomy 6:11-24
- [ ] _____

Thursday:
- [ ] Matthew 5:27-30
- [ ] Colossians 2:16-17
- [ ] _____

Friday:
- [ ] 2 Timothy 3:16-17
- [ ] Matthew 6:33
- [ ] _____

FAST TRACK

Monday:
- [ ] 1 Corinthians 11:32
- [ ] Hebrews 12:11
- [ ] 1 Peter 2:4-12
- [ ] Philippians 2:1-10
- [ ] John 3:1-21

Tuesday:
- [ ] Acts 18:1-21
- [ ] John 8:50-51
- [ ] Acts 20:30
- [ ] 2 Corinthians 6:7
- [ ] James 2:14-26

Wednesday:
- [ ] Matthew 5:17-48
- [ ] Luke 13:3
- [ ] Romans 3:23
- [ ] 1 Peter 2:21-25
- [ ] _____

Thursday:
- [ ] Acts 17:24-25
- [ ] James 2:26
- [ ] Matthew 29:19-20
- [ ] _____
- [ ] _____

Friday:
- [ ] Romans 12:4-6
- [ ] Ephesians 4:1-16
- [ ] Revelation 22:12-15
- [ ] _____
- [ ] _____

Prince James VI of Scotland became King James I of England upon the death of Queen Elizabeth I. In 1604 the Protestant clergy asked the new King for a new translation to replace the Bishop's Bible first printed in 1568. This "translation to end all translations" was the result of the combined efforts of about fifty scholars. They took into consideration: The Tyndale New Testament, The Coverdale Bible, The Matthews Bible, The Great Bible, The Geneva Bible, and even the Rheims New Testament. From 1605 to 1606 the scholars engaged in research. In 1610 the work went to press, and

> **The Booke of John 3:16** For God so loued þe world, that he gaue his only begotten Sonne: that whosoeuer beleeueth in him, should not perish, but haue euerlasting life.
> King James Version

in 1611 the first of the huge 16-inch-tall pulpit editions known today as "The 1611 King James Bible" came off the printing press. Starting just one year after the huge 1611 pulpit-size King James Bibles were printed and chained to every church pulpit in England, printing then began on the earliest normal-size printings of the King James Bible. These were produced so individuals could have their own personal copy of the Bible. The translation is widely considered to be both beautiful and scholarly and thus a towering achievement in English literature.

Growing Panes
No. 510

THIS WEEK'S QUESTION:

BROTHERLY LOVE: *Where is Abel your brother?" And he said, "I do not know. Am I my brother's keeper?"* -
- Genesis 4:9 NASV

DATES

_____ TO _____

INSIDE TRACK

What is Brotherly Love?

How is Brotherly Love Shown?

Examples of Brotherly Love

As a Test of Spirituality

What this Means to us Today

Monday:
- [ ] John 13:34-35

Tuesday:
- [ ] Hebrews 13:1-3

Wednesday:
- [ ] Ephesians 5:1-2

Thursday:
- [ ] Matthew 10:40-42

Friday:
- [ ] Leviticus 19:17-18

MIDDLE LANES

Monday:
- [ ] Mark 12:28-34
- [ ] John 15:9-25
- [ ] Galatians 5:13-16

Tuesday:
- [ ] 1 Corinthians 13:1-13
- [ ] _____
- [ ] _____

Wednesday:
- [ ] 1 John 3:11-24
- [ ] Philippians 1:3-11
- [ ] James 2:1-11

Thursday:
- [ ] Ephesians 1:15-23
- [ ] 1 John 2:3-11
- [ ] Hebrews 6:9-12

Friday:
- [ ] Matthew 5:43-48
- [ ] 1 Peter 1:13-25
- [ ] Matthew 25:34-40

FAST TRACK

Monday:
- [ ] 1 John 5:1-5
- [ ] Matthew 22:34-40
- [ ] Psalm 133:1-3
- [ ] Galatians 6:1-6
- [ ] _____

Tuesday:
- [ ] 1 Thessalonians 4:9-12
- [ ] Luke 10:25-37
- [ ] Romans 13:1-10
- [ ] Philippians 2:1-4
- [ ] John 13:34-35

Wednesday:
- [ ] 1 Thessalonians 5:4-15
- [ ] Romans 14:1-23
- [ ] 2 Thessalonians 1:1-12
- [ ] Colossians 3:12-14
- [ ] 2 Timothy 1:15-18

Thursday:
- [ ] Romans 15:1-9
- [ ] 1 Corinthians 8:1-13
- [ ] Ephesians 4:25-32
- [ ] 2 Peter 1:3-11
- [ ] _____

Friday:
- [ ] 1 Peter 3:8-22
- [ ] 1 John 4:1-21
- [ ] 1 Thessalonians 3:11-13
- [ ] 2 John 1:4-11
- [ ] Leviticus 19:9-18

The King James Bible is held to be the "only" legitimate English language translation for many Protestant denominations, but it is not even a Protestant translation! It was printed to compete with the Protestant Geneva Bible. Those who persecuted and killed Protestants authorized the early KJV'S. The Church of England (the Anglican Church) continued to persecute Protestants throughout the 1600's. One famous example of this is John Bunyan, who wrote *Pilgrim's Progress* while in prison for the crime of preaching the Gospel. Throughout the 1600's, as the

1 Corinthians 13:1 Though I speak with the tongues of men and of angels, and have not charity, I am become *as* sounding brass, or a tinkling cymbal.
King James Version

Puritans and the Pilgrims fled the religious persecution of England to cross the Atlantic and start a new free nation in America, they took with them their precious Geneva Bible, and rejected the King James Bible. The Authorized Version, or King James Version, quickly became the standard for English-speaking Protestants. The flowing language and prose rhythm of the KJV has had a profound influence on the literature of the past 400 years. This version of the Bible became the most widely printed book in history.

Growing Panes
No. 511

THIS WEEK'S QUESTION:

TRUE WORSHIP: *"Come, see a man who told me everything I ever did. Could this be the Christ?"* - John 4:29 Berean Study Bible

	INSIDE TRACK	MIDDLE LANES	FAST TRACK
Lord's Supper/Application	**Monday:** ☐ John 6:35	**Monday:** ☐ Matthew 26:26-29 ☐ Mark 14:22-25 ☐ Acts: 4:42	**Monday:** ☐ 1 Corinthians 10:14-17 ☐ 1 Corinthians 11:17-34 ☐ Acts 20:7-12 ☐ John 6:51-58 ☐ Isaiah 53:1-12
Preaching/Application	**Tuesday:** ☐ Mark 16:15-16	**Tuesday:** ☐ Acts 18:7-9 ☐ Matthew 28-18-20 ☐ 1 Corinthians 14:15-19	**Tuesday:** ☐ 1 Corinthians 2:2-4 ☐ Galatians 1:6-10 ☐ 1 Timothy 4:11-16 ☐ Titus 1:1-4 ☐ 1 Timothy 5:17-18
Singing/Application	**Wednesday:** ☐ Psalm 5:11	**Wednesday:** ☐ Acts 16:25-34 ☐ Matthew 26:30 ☐ Ephesians 5:15-20	**Wednesday:** ☐ Colossians 3:16 ☐ Hebrews 2:11-12 ☐ Psalm 13:5-6 ☐ Romans 15:7-11 ☐ James 5:13
Giving/Application	**Thursday:** ☐ Psalm 37:21	**Thursday:** ☐ Matthew 7:7-12 ☐ 2 Corinthians 9:1-8 ☐ 2 Corinthians 8:1-7	**Thursday:** ☐ James 1:2-8 ☐ Romans 12:6-8 ☐ Acts 5:1-10 ☐ 1 Corinthians 16:1-3 ☐ Matthew 6:2-4
What this Means to us Today	**Friday:** ☐ Psalm 4:1	**Friday:** ☐ Romans 15:30-32 ☐ Acts 12:5-17 ☐ Acts 9:11-19	**Friday:** ☐ John 17:20-26 ☐ Colossians 1:3-14 ☐ Ephesians 6:10-20 ☐ Romans 8:26--27 ☐ 1 Thessalonians 5:16-18

The first Bible printed in America was the native Algonquin Indian Language Bible by John Eliot in 1663. But the first English language Bible to be printed in America was by Robert Aitken in 1782. It was a King James Version. Robert Aitken's 1782 Bible was also the only Bible ever authorized by the United States Congress. He was commended by President George Washington for providing Americans with Bibles during the embargo of imported English goods due to the Revolutionary War. In 1808, Robert's daughter, Jane Aitken, would become the first

> John 6:35 And Jesus said unto them, I am the bread of life: he that cometh to me shall never hunger; and he that believeth on me shall never thirst. King James Version

woman to ever print a Bible... and to do so in America, of course. In 1791, Isaac Collins vastly improved upon the quality and size of the typesetting of American Bibles and produced the first "Family Bible" printed in America... also a King James Version. Also in 1791, Isaiah Thomas published the first Illustrated Bible printed in America...in the King James Version. Just a few years after Noah Webster produced his famous Dictionary of the English Language, he produced his own modern translation of the English Bible in 1833.

Growing Panes

No. 512

What is the *best* translation?

The Bible has been translated into many languages from the biblical languages of Hebrew, Aramaic and Greek. In November of 2014, the full Bible had been translated into 531 languages, and 2,883 languages have at least some portion of the Bible. There seem to be gazillions of translations ranging from the stately King James Version (KJV) to the southern colloquial Cotton Patch Version (CPV) of 1968.

When Hugo McCord (Referenced in Growing Panes No.525A) was asked which was the "best" translation, his answer was "Whichever one you will read and obey." (Now, be sure he believed some passages were incorrectly translated in many versions.) For example, in his first three editions of the McCord translation, he did not use the term "church" but always "congregation." But, he believed the basic truths of God could be gleaned by the diligent student from just about any genuine translation. He also understood that translating is a human attempt to move the original meaning of a word or thought of God from one language to another. The end purpose of all translations should be to convey the original meaning to every generation in a language they will understand.

But, the "BEST" translation is actually not printed, but lived. Like, *"I'd rather <u>see</u> a sermon than to hear one any day!"* The Bible says God became a man in the person of Christ (John 1:1-14). Jesus said, "He who has seen Me has seen the Father" (John 14:9). Jesus translated information about God by "walking among us."

When my dad died, it fell to me and my siblings to go through his belongings and dispose of them. A few things were relatively valuable. Many keepsake items were distributed to his heirs. Most of his meager possessions were sold at auction.

I was granted the privilege of getting his Bibles, including his latest well-worn old KJV. Fifty-three of them! That's right, *fifty-three,* which included many different translations! Most of them were obviously used, but a few were brand new.

Dad loved his Bible. A memory that remains with me is, as a twelve-year-old boy, watching Dad sit in his chair and read his Bible. He always came home for lunch. After eating his lunch, he would go to his chair, get his Bible from the table beside the chair, and read for a time...then, he would take a nap. In fact, it seemed nearly every time he sat down in that chair, the first thing he did was grab his Bible.

But, my monument memory is *how Dad changed* from the time he first started reading his Bible up to the very day he died. The Word was being "formed" (Galatians 4:19) in him. Dad's change came from his faith, which was produced by the Word he read. This changed him.

And we all, who with unveiled faces contemplate the Lord's glory, are being transformed into his image with ever-increasing glory, which comes from the Lord, who is the Spirit. (2 Corinthians 3:18)

I thank God for the clarity of <u>*that*</u> translation! I understood it because I lived with it every day. *That <u>word</u>* (little w) became flesh. That's the <u>*very best*</u> translation!

THIS WEEK'S QUESTION:

LEADERSHIP: *"What were you arguing about on the road?"*

- Mark 9:33b

INSIDE TRACK | MIDDLE LANES | FAST TRACK

Greatness Defined

Christ, the chief Shepherd

Elders, Under-Shepherds

Deacons, Special Servants

What this Means to us Today

INSIDE TRACK

Monday:
- ☐ Deuteronomy 3:24

Tuesday:
- ☐ John 10:27

Wednesday:
- ☐ Titus 1:5

Thursday:
- ☐ Hebrews 6:10

Friday:
- ☐ Philippians 2:3-4

MIDDLE LANES

Monday:
- ☐ Psalm 145:1-21
- ☐ 1 Chronicles 29:10-13
- ☐ _____

Tuesday:
- ☐ Psalm 23:1-6
- ☐ Luke 15:1-7
- ☐ Psalm 100:1-6

Wednesday:
- ☐ 1 Peter 5:1-10
- ☐ Acts 14:21-23
- ☐ Hebrews 13:17

Thursday:
- ☐ Matthew 25:31-46
- ☐ Romans 12:3-13
- ☐ Galatians 5:13-15

Friday:
- ☐ Luke 12:41-47
- ☐ Luke 6:27-36
- ☐ Ephesians 6:5-9

FAST TRACK

Monday:
- ☐ Matthew 18:1-5
- ☐ Jeremiah 32:17-19
- ☐ Deuteronomy 10:14-22
- ☐ Mark 10:35-45
- ☐ Job 36:22-33

Tuesday:
- ☐ John 10:1-18
- ☐ Ezekiel 34:23-31
- ☐ Revelation 7:15-17
- ☐ 1 Peter 2:21-25
- ☐ Hebrews 13:7-21

Wednesday:
- ☐ 1 Timothy 3:1-7
- ☐ Titus 1:5-9
- ☐ 1 Timothy 5:17-18
- ☐ Acts 20:28-32
- ☐ James 5:14

Thursday:
- ☐ Philippians 2:1-11
- ☐ 1 Timothy 3:8-13
- ☐ Acts 6:1-7
- ☐ John 13:12-17
- ☐ Matthew 20:20-28

Friday:
- ☐ Exodus 18:7-26
- ☐ Psalm 78:70-72
- ☐ 1 Kings 3:7-15
- ☐ Colossians 3:18-25
- ☐ Proverb 3:5-10

The first modern English translation of the Bible was the English Revised Version (1881-1894). It was a British revision of the King James Version (KJV) of 1611. The New Testament was published in 1881, the Old Testament in 1885, and the Apocrypha was added in 1894. It was the first and remains the only officially authorized and recognized revision of the King James Version in Britain. The work was entrusted to over 50 scholars from various denominations in Britain. While the text of the translation itself is widely regarded as excessively literal and flat, the Revised Version is significant in the history of English Bible translation for many reasons. At the time of the RV's publication, the nearly 300-year-old King James Version was still the only viable English Bible in Victorian England. The RV, therefore, is regarded as the forerunner of the entire modern translation tradition. And it was considered more accurate than the King James Version in a number of verses. Another curious characteristic of this translation was the absence of the 14 Apocryphal books. Up until the 1880's every Protestant Bible (not just Catholic Bibles) had 80 books.

> Deuteronomy 3:24 O Lord GOD, thou hast begun to shew thy servant thy greatness, and thy strong hand: for what god is there in heaven or in earth, that can do according to thy works, and according to thy mighty acts? English Revised Version

Growing Panes
No. 513

THIS WEEK'S QUESTION:

UNITY: *"Is Christ divided?"* - 1 Corinthians 1:13 NIV

Topics	INSIDE TRACK	MIDDLE LANES	FAST TRACK
Unity of God's People	**Monday:** ☐ John 17:20-23	**Monday:** ☐ 1 Corinthians 12:12-31 ☐ Ephesians 1:3-10 ☐ Ephesians 4:3-16	**Monday:** ☐ Psalm 133 ☐ Romans 12:1-21 ☐ 1 Corinthians 1:9-17 ☐ Romans 16: 17-20 ☐ _____
Causes of Division	**Tuesday:** ☐ James 4:1	**Tuesday:** ☐ James 4:2-12 ☐ Matthew 7:16-23 ☐ _____	**Tuesday:** ☐ 1 Corinthians 3:1-23 ☐ Jude 1:3-4, 16-19 ☐ 1 Corinthians 11:18-19 ☐ 2 Peter 2:1-3 ☐ Colossians 3:13
Remedies for Division	**Wednesday:** ☐ Ephesians 4:32	**Wednesday:** ☐ Ephesians 4:15 ☐ Titus 2:11-13 ☐ _____	**Wednesday:** ☐ Galatians 5:19-23 ☐ 1 Peter 4:8-11 ☐ Matthew 18:15-20 ☐ Matthew 10:1-40 ☐ _____
Being United	**Thursday:** ☐ Ephesians 4:1	**Thursday:** ☐ Galatians 3:26-28 ☐ Ephesians 4:2-6 ☐ _____	**Thursday:** ☐ 1 Peter 5:8-22 ☐ Ephesians 2:11-22 ☐ Philippians 2:3 ☐ Titus 3:10 ☐ _____
What this Means to us Today	**Friday:** ☐ Philippians 4: 4	**Friday:** ☐ Philippians 4: 1-9 ☐ 1 Thessalonians 5:1-18 ☐ Psalm 118: 22-24	**Friday:** ☐ 1 Chronicles 29:10-20 ☐ Psalm 119:73-80 ☐ Romans 5:1-8 ☐ Philippians 4:10-13 ☐ _____

The Americans responded to England's ERV Bible by publishing the nearly-identical American Standard Version (ASV) in 1901. It was also widely accepted and embraced by churches throughout America for many decades as the leading modern-English version of the Bible. In 1971, it was again revised and called New American Standard Version Bible (often referred to as the NASV or NASB. or NAS.). This New American Standard Bible is considered by many conservative Christian scholars and translators today, to be the most accurate, word-for-word translation of the original

Ephesians 4:1-2 Therefore I, the prisoner of the Lord, implore you to walk in a manner worthy of the calling with which you have been called,
New American Standard Bible

Greek and Hebrew scriptures into the modern English language that has ever been produced. Some, however, have taken issue with it because it is so direct and literal a translation (focused on accuracy), that it does not flow as easily in conversational English. In 1995, the text of the NASB was updated for greater understanding and smoother reading. The original NASB has earned the reputation of being the most accurate English Bible translation. The NASB update is a true Bible translation, revealing what the original manuscripts actually say--not merely what the translator believes they mean.

Growing Panes
No. 514

THIS WEEK'S QUESTION:

BACKSLIDING: *"Do you want to go away as well?"*

- John 6:67 ESV

DATES
_____ TO _____

INSIDE TRACK | MIDDLE LANES | FAST TRACK

Danger of Backsliding

Causes of Backsliding

Conditions of Backsliders

Restoring Backsliders

What this Means to us Today

INSIDE TRACK	MIDDLE LANES	FAST TRACK
Monday:	**Monday:**	**Monday:**
☐ Hebrews 3:12	☐ 1 Corinthians 10:1-24	☐ Ephesians 5:1-20
	☐ Hebrews 3:7-19	☐ 1 Timothy 6:11-21
	☐ Proverb 14:14	☐ Hebrews 3:12-19
		☐ _____
		☐ _____
Tuesday:	**Tuesday:**	**Tuesday:**
☐ Matthew 24:12-13	☐ Galatians 4:8-20	☐ Exodus 32:1-14
	☐ John 6:66-69	☐ Ephesians 4:17-32
	☐ 1 Timothy 6:3-10	☐ Matthew 13:18-23
		☐ Matthew 8:12-14
		☐ Isaiah 59:12-15
Wednesday:	**Wednesday:**	**Wednesday:**
☐ Isaiah 1:4	☐ Isaiah 1:1-17	☐ Jeremiah 14:10-22
	☐ Jeremiah 14:7-10	☐ Malachi 3:6-18
	☐ 1 Timothy 4:1-5	☐ Luke 15:11-24
		☐ 2 Kings 17:7-15
		☐ _____
Thursday:	**Thursday:**	**Thursday:**
☐ James 5:19-20	☐ John 21:1-22	☐ 2 Corinthians 2:1-11
	☐ Luke 22:54-62	☐ Isaiah 55:6-9
	☐ 1 John 1:5-10	☐ Jeremiah 4 :1-4
		☐ 1 Corinthians 5:1-13
		☐ Matthew 18:10-22
Friday:	**Friday:**	**Friday:**
☐ Hebrews 13:17	☐ Hebrews 10:19-39	☐ 2 Timothy 4:1-22
	☐ 2 Peter 2:17-22	☐ 2 Timothy 2:4-26
	☐ 1 Peter 5:1-9	☐ John 12:44-50
		☐ 1 John 2:14-17
		☐ _____

The **REVISED STANDARD VERSION (RSV)** First published in 1946 in the New Testament and 1952 in the Old Testament, it has received mixed reviews due to several unfortunate translations of key verses such as Isaiah where "young woman" is used rather than "virgin." Charges of liberalism have also been lodged because the copyright is owned by the National Council of Churches. The Committee translating the RSV noted, "The Revised Standard Version Bible seeks to preserve all that is best in the English Bible as it has been known and used through the years." In 1989, the National Council of Church-

Hebrews 13:17 Obey your leaders and submit to them; for they are keeping watch over your souls, as men who will have to give account. Let them do this joyfully, and not sadly, for that would be of no advantage to you. Revised Standard Version

es released a full-scale revision to the RSV called the New *Revised Standard Version.* It was the first major version to use gender-neutral language, and drew even more criticism from conservative Christians than did its 1952 predecessor. Overall, the *Revised Standard Version* was a good English Bible translation in its time. The RSV, though, can no longer be said to be a modern English translation. While it is more "modern" than the KJV, it does not read as English is spoken today. The RSV is a good balance between formal equivalency and dynamic equivalency, more so than its successor, the NRSV.

Growing Panes

No. 515

No. 516

THIS WEEK'S QUESTION:

SINS OF TONGUE: *" Can both fresh water and salt water flow from the same spring?"*

- *James 3:10-11 World English Bible*

WEEK 16

DATES
_____ TO _____

Gossip and Slander		

INSIDE TRACK | MIDDLE LANES | FAST TRACK

Gossip and Slander	**Monday:**	**Monday:**	**Monday:**
	☐ James 4:11-12	☐ Psalm 10:3-5	☐ 3 John 9-10
		☐ Psalm 50:16-22	☐ Proverb 10:18-20
		☐ Jeremiah 9:1-11	☐ 2 Corinthians 12:19-21
			☐ Psalm 52:1-9
			☐ _____
Faultfinding and Judgment	**Tuesday:**	**Tuesday:**	**Tuesday:**
	☐ Matthew 17:15-17	☐ Romans 2:1-11	☐ Romans 14:1-22
		☐ Matthew 7:1-6	☐ James 1: 26-27
		☐ _____	☐ 1 Corinthians 4:1-5
			☐ Ephesians 4:25-32
			☐
Lying	**Wednesday:**	**Wednesday:**	**Wednesday:**
	☐ Leviticus 19:11	☐ Psalm 34:11-14	☐ 1 John 4:19-21
		☐ 1 Peter 3:8-12	☐ 1 John 2:1-6
		☐ Psalm 120:1-7	☐ Psalm 58:1-5
			☐ Ezekiel 13:8-9
			☐ _____
Critical and Contentious	**Thursday:**	**Thursday:**	**Thursday:**
	☐ Titus 3:1-2	☐ Proverb 12:13-23	☐ Proverb 25:2-28
		☐ 2 Timothy 2:22-26	☐ Galatians 5:14-15
		☐ Romans 12:18-21	☐ Titus 3:9-11
			☐ _____
			☐ _____
What this Means to us Today	**Friday:**	**Friday:**	**Friday:**
	☐ Leviticus 19:15-17	☐ Matthew 12:33-37	☐ 1 Timothy 5:11-15
		☐ Luke 6:41-42	☐ Proverb 16:27-30
		☐ 1 Corinthians 13:1-13	☐ James 3:3-12
			☐ _____
			☐ _____

I n 1973, the New International Version (NIV) was produced, which was offered as a "dynamic equivalent" translation into modern English. The NIV was designed not for "word-for-word" accuracy, but rather, for "phrase-for-phrase" accuracy, and ease of reading. It was meant to appeal to a broader (and in some instances less-educated) cross-section of the general public. Critics often jokingly refer to it as the "Nearly Inspired Version," but almost 50 years after the vision was cast—and more than 450 million copies later, the NIV is the most widely read Bible translation in contem-

James 3:6 The tongue also is a fire, a world of evil among the parts of the body. It corrupts the whole body, sets the whole course of one's life on fire, and is itself set on fire by hell. New International Version

porary English. The NIV translators were united by their conviction that the Bible is God's inspired Word. The NIV was translated by an independent, self-governing team of Bible scholars. No publisher, commercial or otherwise, could tell them how to translate God's Word. The translators came from dozens of denominations and churches, and they can only make changes to the text if 70% of the committee agrees — safeguarding against theological bias. Originally published in the 1970s, the NIV was updated in 1984 and 2011.

Growing Panes

No. 516

THIS WEEK'S QUESTION:

OUR FEARS: *"Why are you so afraid? Do you still have no faith?"* -*Mark 4:40 NASV*

DATES _____ TO _____

INSIDE TRACK / MIDDLE LANES / FAST TRACK

Fear of the Unknown

Fear of Death

Our Hope in Christ

Our Faith for Life After Death

What this Means to us Today

INSIDE TRACK

Monday:
- [ ] Luke 2:8-9

Tuesday:
- [ ] Psalm 23:4

Wednesday:
- [ ] Romans 15:13

Thursday:
- [ ] James 2:5

Friday:
- [ ] John 20:30-31

MIDDLE LANES

Monday:
- [ ] Psalm 91:5-16
- [ ] Matthew 27:50-54
- [ ] Luke 1:8-17

Tuesday:
- [ ] 1 Samuel 5:10-12
- [ ] Jonah 1:4-16
- [ ] Acts 27:21-32

Wednesday:
- [ ] John 14:23-31
- [ ] Romans 15:4-13
- [ ] 1 John 5:11-20

Thursday:
- [ ] John 3:10-21
- [ ] Hebrews 11:6-10
- [ ] Jude vss. 17-25

Friday:
- [ ] Romans 8:28-39
- [ ] 1 John 4:13-21
- [ ] 2 Peter 3:8-13

FAST TRACK

Monday:
- [ ] Matthew 17:1-8
- [ ] Mark 6:45-52
- [ ] Mark 16:1-8
- [ ] Luke 2:8-15
- [ ] Luke 8:26-37

Tuesday:
- [ ] Psalm 55:4-8
- [ ] Jeremiah 26:20-23
- [ ] Mark 4:35-41
- [ ] Luke 12:4-12
- [ ] Hebrews 2:14-18

Wednesday:
- [ ] 1 John 3:1-3
- [ ] Acts 24:14-16
- [ ] Acts 26:4-8
- [ ] Colossians 1:15-23
- [ ] 1 Peter 3:13-22

Thursday:
- [ ] Acts 14:21-22
- [ ] Acts 26:12-18
- [ ] Romans 6:19-23
- [ ] Ephesians 2:4-10
- [ ] 1 Peter 1:3-9

Friday:
- [ ] 1 Cor. 15:12-22, 50-58
- [ ] Philippians 3:7-14
- [ ] 2 Timothy 4:16-18
- [ ] Hebrews 6:9-12
- [ ] Isaiah 40:28-31

The goal of any Bible translation is to convey the **meaning** of the ancient Hebrew and Greek texts as accurately as possible to the modern reader. Thus, every generation since Wycliffe has produced new English versions. The challenge for the New Living Translation was to create a text that would make the same **impact** in the life of modern readers that the original text had for the original readers. This is accomplished by translating **entire thoughts** into natural, everyday English. The result is a translation that is easy to read and understand and that accurately communicates the meaning of the original text. It has been suggested that this "thought-for-thought" methodology is less accurate than a literal (formal equivalence) method, and thus the New Living Translation may not be suitable for those wishing to undertake detailed study of the Bible. The translators started out to simply revise the The Living Bible. Work on this revision began in 1989 with ninety translators and published in July 1996. The NLT is second only to the NIV in unit sales.

Psalm 23:4 Even when I walk through the darkest valley, I will not be afraid, for you are close beside me. New Living Translation

Growing Panes
No. 517

THIS WEEK'S QUESTION:

CITIZENSHIP: *"Is it lawful to pay taxes to Caesar, or not?"* - Mark 12:14 Holman Christian Standard Bible

INSIDE TRACK | MIDDLE LANES | FAST TRACK

God and Government

INSIDE TRACK	MIDDLE LANES	FAST TRACK
Monday:	**Monday:**	**Monday:**
☐ 1 Timothy 2:1-3	☐ Acts 4:17-21	☐ Luke 20:19-26
	☐ Titus 3:1-2	☐ Romans 13:1-10
	☐ Matthew 22:15-22	☐ _____
		☐ _____
		☐ _____

Duties to the State

Tuesday:	**Tuesday:**	**Tuesday:**
☐ Luke 2:1-5	☐ 2 Kings 23:33-37	☐ Ezra 6:3-22
	☐ Titus 2:11-3:2	☐ Ezra 7:6-28
	☐ _____	☐ _____
		☐ _____
		☐ _____

Duties to God

Wednesday:	**Wednesday:**	**Wednesday:**
☐ 3 John vss. 11-12	☐ Matthew 6:1-15	☐ Hebrews 12:14-29
	☐ Titus 2:11	☐ Hebrews 13:1-6
	☐ Psalm 19:1-12	☐ _____
		☐ _____
		☐ _____

Christian Service to Others

Thursday:	**Thursday:**	**Thursday:**
☐ John 13:1-5	☐ Luke 10:23-37	☐ Psalm 89:1-21
	☐ 2 Kings 5:1-15	☐ 2 Samuel 9:1-13
	☐ _____	☐ John 3:16-21
		☐ _____
		☐ _____

What this Means to us Today

Friday:	**Friday:**	**Friday:**
☐ 1 Peter 5:5-7	☐ 2 Peter 1:4-8	☐ 3 John 5-6
	☐ Ruth 2:7-14	☐ 1 John 5:13-15
	☐ _____	☐ Joshua 3—Joshua 4
		☐ _____
		☐ _____

J.B. Phillips (1906-1982), was well known within the Church of England for his commitment to making the message of truth relevant to today's world. Phillips' translation of the New Testament brings home the full force of the original message. *The New Testament in Modern English* was originally written for the benefit of Phillips' youth group; it was later published more widely in response to popular demand. Phillips began by rewording the New Testament epistles for his church's youth group in modern English, which group met during World War II in bomb shelters. These he published in 1947 under the title *Letters to Young Churches*. In 1952 he added the Gospels. In 1955 he added Acts and titled it *The Young Church in Action*. In 1957 he added *The Book of Revelation*. Later he finished the whole of the New Testament, first publishing it in 1958, revising it and republishing it in 1961 and 1972. Phillips worked entirely from the Greek Testament. The best known, and often quoted, passage from the translation is a portion of Romans 12:2, "Don't let the world around you squeeze you into its own mould."

John 3:16 For God loved the world so much that he gave his only Son, so that every one who believes in him shall not be lost, but should have eternal life. Phillips Translation

Growing Panes
No. 518

S aving truth or killing error! Which?

"Beware! Danger at the Doctor" by Fox News anchor Bill Hemmer on June 26, 2016 reported on a study by John Hopkins researchers who estimated that 251,454 people fall victim to medical errors each year! This is the third leading cause of death in the U. S. only behind heart disease and cancer. That's like wiping out the entire population of Orlando, Florida *each year!* Combine all annual deaths from guns, suicide, and car accidents, double them, and it is still less than die from medical error.

Alarming! Who of us would expect or want to be one of those statistics? We wonder if we can trust either the medical practices or the doctors who care for our physical health. It *is* a matter of life or death! But, Bible students are reminded of the words of Jesus:

> *Do not be afraid of those who kill the body but cannot kill the soul. Rather, be afraid of the One who can destroy both soul and body in hell.* (Matthew 10:28 NIV).

The truth "will set you free" from the spiritual disease of sin (John 8:32). The Bible says you will "die in your sins" unless you accept the faith of Jesus (John 8:23-24). When we know we are spiritually sick, we ask the haunting question, "Men and brethren, what shall we do (Acts 2:37)?" The disease is sin. It is terminal unless treated (Romans 3:23). Like the Philippian jailer (Acts 16:29), we want to know the truth that will set us free from this dreaded disease!

What we *don't want* is to become the victim of a spiritual medical error! Neither do we want "think-so's" and "maybe's"! The truth, and the truth *only!* Nothing else is important.

Alexander Campbell, translator of the *Living Oracles* version and early church restoration leader, was faced with a major translation issue when his daughter was born on March 13, 1812. Should she be baptized according to their Presbyterian faith? He, his father Thomas, and members of the Brush Run congregation began an intense study of baptism. Thomas Campbell, with a dedicated history as a Presbyterian minister, resisted what they concluded: *The Bible teaches that baptism is not for infants, but for believers.*

David Noah Bryant, a member of the group said, "Elder Campbell, if we are going to follow only the truth, then you must be baptized." They had already committed to follow only what was taught in the Bible. Their theme was to become: "Where the Bible speaks, we speak; where the Bible is silent, we will be silent."

On June 12, 1812 Alexander Campbell, his father and mother, his wife, and several members of the group were baptized in a "deep hole on Buffalo Creek" near the property of David Bryant. The next day thirteen more were baptized.

The meaning of a Greek word like βάπτισμα, "baptism" is important. It means "to dip, to plunge, to immerse." The original meaning must be translated to match the same meaning words for every generation. This is just one example of why it is important that we know the truth, translated into language we can understand. It's a matter of life and death!

THIS WEEK'S QUESTION:

LOVE: *"Simon son of John, do you love me more than these?"* - John 21:15 NIV

Love Described	**INSIDE TRACK**	**MIDDLE LANES**	**FAST TRACK**
	Monday:	**Monday:**	**Monday:**
	☐ 1 John 4: 16	☐ John 3:13-18	☐ John 15:5-15
		☐ Romans 5:6-10	☐ Romans 13:8-14
		☐ 1 John 5:1-5	☐ 1 Corinthians 13:4-8
			☐ Colossians 3:12-17
			☐ _____
Love of Jesus	**Tuesday:**	**Tuesday:**	**Tuesday:**
	☐ John 13:1	☐ John 14:28-31	☐ John 11:1-3
		☐ Romans 8:38-39	☐ Titus 3:3-8
		☐ Philippians 2:1-3	☐ John 15:9-17
			☐ Ephesians 3:14-19
			☐ Ephesians 1:4-10
Love Jesus	**Wednesday:**	**Wednesday:**	**Wednesday:**
	☐ Matthew 22:37-40	☐ John 21:10-17	☐ Matthew 25:31-46
		☐ John 14:21-24	☐ Mark 12:32-34
		☐ Ephesians 6:23-24	☐ John 6:60-69
			☐ 1 John 4:16-21
			☐ _____
Love Others	**Thursday:**	**Thursday:**	**Thursday:**
	☐ Matthew 7:12	☐ John 13:33-35	☐ Ephesians 4:1-3
		☐ Romans 12:9-13	☐ 1 Peter 1:22-25
		☐ Galatians 5:13-23	☐ _____
			☐ _____
			☐ _____
What this Means to us Today	**Friday:**	**Friday:**	**Friday:**
	☐ Ephesians 5:1-2	☐ Ephesians 5:15-33	☐ Proverb 3:1-27
		☐ Revelation 2:1-7	☐ Proverb 16:6-9
		☐ _____	☐ Psalm 116:1-7
			☐ 2 Corinthians 5:14-21
			☐ _____

The New English Bible (NEB) with the Apocrypha came out in 1970. In May of 1946, it was determined that a new translation should be undertaken in order to produce a Bible with thoroughly "modern English." The editor of this project with a 25-member team of translators was C. H. Dodd. Work began soon thereafter, and the New Testament was published in 1961 with the whole Bible appearing in 1970. It was significantly revised and re-published in

Romans 8:38-39 For I am convinced that there is nothing in death or life, in the realm of spirits or superhuman powers, in the world as it is or the world as it shall be, in the forces of the universe, in heights or depths- nothing in all creation that can separate us from the love of God in Christ Jesus our Lord.

New English Bible

1989 as the *Revised English Bible.* In more than one way it resembles the earlier Moffatt Bible with its free translation style. The translators used great freedom with the original texts. The *New English Bible* never gained wide acceptance, either in England or the United States. While it is an adequate translation, there was nothing "special" about it that would attract people to use it as their primary Bible.

Growing Panes

No. 519

THIS WEEK'S QUESTION:

FORGIVENESS: *Lord, how oft shall my brother sin against me, and I forgive him? till seven times?* - Matthew 18:21 ASV

DATES
_____ TO _____

	INSIDE TRACK	**MIDDLE LANES**	**FAST TRACK**
Forgiveness in the Old Testament	**Monday:** ☐ Leviticus 4:20	**Monday:** ☐ Numbers 14:1-20 ☐ Leviticus 5:14-16 ☐ Leviticus 5:17-19	**Monday:** ☐ Numbers 15:22-31 ☐ Leviticus 5:7-10 ☐ Leviticus 6:1-6 ☐ ☐
Forgiveness in the Gospels	**Tuesday:** ☐ Matthew 9:1-2	**Tuesday:** ☐ Mark 2:1-11 ☐ Mark 3:23-29 ☐ Matthew 18:23-35	**Tuesday:** ☐ John 8:1-11 ☐ John 8:23-24 ☐ Luke 7:44-48 ☐ Mark 11:25 ☐ _____
Results of Disobeying	**Wednesday:** ☐ Joshua 24:19-20	**Wednesday:** ☐ Exodus 23:20-26 ☐ Exodus 32:30-35 ☐ Hosea 1:1-7	**Wednesday:** ☐ Jeremiah 5:1-9 ☐ Jeremiah 18:19-23 ☐ 2 Kings 24:1-4 ☐ Micah 7:18-20 ☐ _____
Obeying the Lord	**Thursday:** ☐ Matthew 6:14-15	**Thursday:** ☐ Luke 11:1-4 ☐ Luke 23:32-34 ☐ John 20:21-23	**Thursday:** ☐ Matthew 12:30-32 ☐ Luke 6:37-38 ☐ Luke 1:76-79 ☐ Matthew 18:15-17 ☐ Luke 5:17-20
What this Means to us Today	**Friday:** ☐ Matthew 26:28-29	**Friday:** ☐ Luke 24:46-49 ☐ Acts 10:39-43 ☐ Luke 23:43	**Friday:** ☐ Hebrews 9:15-28 ☐ 2 Corinthians 2:5-11 ☐ Acts 2:36-38 ☐ 1 John 1:5-10 ☐ Colossians 1:13-14

In 2002, a major attempt was made to bridge the gap between the simple readability of the NIV, and the extremely precise accuracy of the NASB. This translation is called the English Standard Version (ESV) and is rapidly gaining popularity for its readability and accuracy. It is an updating of the Revised Standard Version of 1971. It should be placed in the mainstream of classic English Bibles (KJV, RV, ASV, and RSV). In that stream, faithfulness to the text and vigorous pursuit of accuracy were combined

Matthew 6:14-15 For if you forgive others their trespasses, your heavenly Father will also forgive you, but if you do not forgive others their trespasses, neither will your Father forgive your trespasses. English Standard Version

with simplicity, beauty, and dignity of expression. The strength of the ESV is its combination of formal adherence to the text of Scripture and beauty of language. The ESV uses some gender-neutral language such as "person" or "one" instead of "man." If one is looking for a balanced combination of scholarship in translation and fluency of language, one might consider this version. The hundred-member translating team shared a common commitment to the truth of God's Word and to historic Christian orthodoxy.

Growing Panes

No. 520

THIS WEEK'S QUESTION:

RESURRECTION: *"If a man dies, shall he live again?"*

- Job 14:14 English Revised Version

WEEK 21

DATES
_____ TO _____

INSIDE TRACK	MIDDLE LANES	FAST TRACK

Certifies our Salvation

Monday:
☐ 1 Corinthians 15:1-2

Monday:
☐ 1 Corinthians 15:3-33
☐ 1 Peter 1:3-12
☐ Luke 14:1-14

Monday:
☐ Romans 4:18-25
☐ Luke 24:1-53
☐ _____
☐ _____
☐ _____

Demonstrates God's Power

Tuesday:
☐ John 11:25

Tuesday:
☐ 1 Corinthians 15:35-57
☐ Colossians 2:6-15
☐ Romans 8:1-17

Tuesday:
☐ John 6:25-59
☐ John 2:13-22
☐ Philippians 3:1-21
☐ _____
☐ _____

Gives us Hope after Death

Wednesday:
☐ Romans 8:28

Wednesday:
☐ Romans 8:18-30
☐ 1 Thessalonians 4:13-18
☐ _____

Wednesday:
☐ Romans 8:31-39
☐ Ezekiel 37:1-14
☐ Psalm 16:1-11
☐ John 14:1-13
☐ _____

Demands our Loyalty

Thursday:
☐ 1 Corinthians 15:58

Thursday:
☐ Revelation 1:9-18
☐ Daniel 12:1-4
☐ Isaiah 26:19-21

Thursday:
☐ John 5:16-28
☐ Acts 23:1-10
☐ 2 Timothy 2:14-26
☐ Philippians 1:12-29
☐ _____

What this Means to us Today

Friday:
☐ Romans 8:37

Friday:
☐ John 11:1-44
☐ Matthew 10:5-32
☐ _____

Friday:
☐ Mark 16:9-20
☐ Ephesians 1:15-22
☐ Matthew 22:23-33
☐ Luke 20:27-47
☐ Ecclesiastes 12:1-14

The Message New Testament (2002) translated by Eugene Peterson attempts to capture the tone of the text and the original conversational feel of the Greek, in contemporary English. In his words, *"While I was teaching a class on Galatians, I began to realize that the adults in my class weren't feeling the vitality and directness that I sensed as I read and studied the New Testament in its original Greek. I hoped to bring the New Testament to life for two different types of people: those who hadn't read the Bible because it seemed too distant and irrelevant and those who had read the Bible so much that it had become 'old hat.'"* He decided to strive for the spirit of the original manuscripts to express the rhythm of

1 Corinthians 15:58 With all this going for us, my dear, dear friends, stand your ground. And don't hold back. Throw yourselves into the work of the Master, confident that nothing you do for him is a waste of time or effort.   The Message

the voices, the flavor of the idiomatic expressions, the subtle connotations of meaning that are often lost in English translations. The goal of The Message is to engage people in the reading process and help them understand what they read. This is not a study Bible, but rather "a reading Bible." The verse numbers have been left out to facilitate easy and enjoyable reading. The Message tries to recapture the Word in the words we use today. *The Message* is not truly a translation, nor can it strictly be said to be a paraphrase of the original languages of the Bible.

Growing Panes
No. 521

THIS WEEK'S QUESTION:

JUDGMENT: *"Far be it from you to do such a thing. . .The Judge of all the earth will do what is right, won't he?"*
Genesis 18:25 International Standard Version

WEEK 22

DATES
_____ TO _____

The Judgment of God	**INSIDE TRACK**	**MIDDLE LANES**	**FAST TRACK**
	Monday:	**Monday**	**Monday**
	☐ Genesis 10:25	☐ Genesis 18:16-33	☐ Deuteronomy 1:13-18
		☐ John 16:7-9	☐ John 5:21-31
		☐ Revelation 19:1-3	☐ Ecclesiastes 12:14
			☐ Hebrews 9:27
			☐ _____
Who will be Judged	**Tuesday:**	**Tuesday**	**Tuesday**
	☐ Exodus 6:6	☐ 2 Chronicles 19:8	☐ John 9:38-39
		☐ Proverb 20:7-9	☐ Psalm 97:8
		☐ Romans 13:1-3	☐ John 12:38-39
			☐ John 12:30-32
			☐ _____
Basis of Judgment	**Wednesday:**	**Wednesday**	**Wednesday**
	☐ Exodus 12:12	☐ Matthew 7:2-4	☐ 1 John 2:1-29
		☐ Romans 14:1-4	☐ Revelation 20:11-15
		☐ 2 Corinthians 5:10	☐ James 4:4
			☐ Matthew 25:31-34
			☐ _____
Alternatives of Judgment	**Thursday:**	**Thursday**	**Thursday**
	☐ Psalm 51:4	☐ 1 Corinthians 4:5	☐ Romans 5:1-21
		☐ 1 Peter 4:17	☐ Isaiah 53:1-12
		☐ Romans 14:12-14	☐ Matthew 12:36-37
			☐ John 8:24
			☐ Matthew 25:45-46
What this Means to us Today	**Friday:**	**Friday**	**Friday**
	☐ Psalm 74:6-7	☐ John 3:18	☐ John 3:16
		☐ Ezekiel 9:1-11	☐ Psalm 32:1-11
		☐ Romans 2:1-5	☐ Matthew 13:47-50
			☐ Matthew 13:39-43
			☐ Daniel 7:9-10

2 Corinthians 5:10 For all of us must appear before Christ, to be judged by him. We will each receive what we deserve, according to everything we have done, good or bad, in our bodily life. Good News Translation

The Good News Translation (GNT), formerly called the Good News Bible or Today's English Version, was first published as a full Bible in 1976 by the American Bible Society as a "common language" Bible. It is a clear and simple modern translation that is faithful to the original Hebrew, Koine Greek, and Aramaic texts. The GNT is a highly trusted version.

It first appeared in New Testament form in 1966 as *Good News for Modern Man: The New Testament in Today's English Version*, translated by Dr. Robert G. Bratcher in consultation with a committee appointed by the American Bible Society. First titled *Good News for Modern Man: The New Testament in Today's English Version*, it was released in 1966 as a 599-page paperback with a publication date of January 1, 1966. It is a "thought-for-thought" translation rather than a "word-for-word". This approach became known as a "dynamic equivalence" translation. In 1991 polls showed that it was one of the most popular English versions.

Growing Panes
No. 522

THIS WEEK'S QUESTION:

PERSEVERANCE: *His wife asked him, "Are you still holding on to your principles? Curse God and die!"* - Job 2:9 God's Word Translation

Enemies of Perseverance	**INSIDE TRACK**	**MIDDLE LANES**	**FAST TRACK**
	Monday:	**Monday:**	**Monday:**
	☐ 1 John 2:15	☐ Job 27:1-23	☐ Joshua 23:1-16
		☐ 1 John 2:16-17	☐ Deuteronomy 8:11-20
		☐ _____	☐ James 5:1-6
			☐ 2 Corinthians 4:1-18
			☐ _____
Preparations to Persevere	**Tuesday:**	**Tuesday:**	**Tuesday:**
	☐ Hebrews 12:3	☐ Luke 18:1-8	☐ Colossians 3:5-17
		☐ Job 23:10	☐ James 1:13-15
		☐ 1 Corinthians 15:50-58	☐ Ephesians 6:10-20
			☐ John 8:31-47
			☐ 1 Peter 5:8
Trials and Temptations	**Wednesday:**	**Wednesday:**	**Wednesday:**
	☐ James 4:7	☐ Luke 4:1-12	☐ Acts 14:21-25
		☐ Hebrews 2:17-18	☐ James 1:2-14
		☐ _____	☐ 1 Corinthians 10:12-13
			☐ Romans 5:1-11
			☐ _____
Power to Stand	**Thursday:**	**Thursday:**	**Thursday:**
	☐ Matthew 6:13	☐ Daniel 3:8-30	☐ 1 Corinthians 4:1-8
		☐ Isaiah 48:10	☐ Galatians 5:16-26
		☐ John 11:17-37	☐ I Timothy 4:1-11
			☐ Psalm 66:10
			☐ _____
What this Means to us Today	**Friday:**	**Friday:**	**Friday:**
	☐ Galatians 6:9	☐ Job 42:7-17	☐ Proverb 3:1-12
		☐ Galatians 5:1-12	☐ Psalm 1:1-6
		☐ _____	☐ Philippians 4:8-9
			☐ Matthew 25:1-12
			☐ 1 Timothy 4:12-16

The Modern English Version (MEV) heralds a new day for Bibles with the most modern translation ever produced in the King James tradition, providing fresh clarity for Bible readers everywhere with an updated language that doesn't compromise the truth of the original texts. The MEV maintains the beauty of the past, yet provides clarity for a new generation of Bible readers. The MEV is a literal translation. It is also often referred to as a formal equivalence translation. The translation committee began its work on the MEV in 2005 and completed it in 2014.   The chief editor is James F. Linzey, who conceived

> John 11:25-26 Jesus said to her, "I am the resurrection and the life. He who believes in Me, though he may die, yet shall he live. And whoever lives and believes in Me shall never die. Do you believe this?" Modern English Version

the MEV and was assisted by 47 translators from Protestant and Catholic traditions.

The Committee re-translated the *Textus Receptus* and the *Masoretic Text*, using the KJV as a reference. Thus, the format and translation style is very similar to the KJV without many of the archaic language issues of the KJV. The MEV, therefore, is an updated edition of the KJV in a more modern English vernacular. Bible students who love the rhythm and poetry of the KJV will appreciate the MEV.

Growing Panes

No. 523

THIS WEEK'S QUESTION:

MARRIAGE: *"In the resurrection, therefore, whose wife of the seven will she be? For they all had married her."* - Matthew 22:28 NET BIBLE

INSIDE TRACK

Biblical Marriage

Monday:
- [ ] Proverb 18:22

Duties in Marriage

Tuesday:
- [ ] Hebrews 13:4

Marriage and Family

Wednesday:
- [ ] Proverb 21:9

Old Testament on Marriage

Thursday:
- [ ] Proverb 31:10

What this Means to us Today

Friday:
- [ ] Genesis 1:27

MIDDLE LANES

Monday:
- [ ] Genesis 2:15-25
- [ ] Matthew 19:1-11
- [ ] 1 Corinthians 7:1-40

Tuesday:
- [ ] 1 Peter 3:1-12
- [ ] Ephesians 5:21-33
- [ ] 1 Corinthians 11:1-6

Wednesday:
- [ ] Malachi 2:13-26
- [ ] 1 Kings 11:1-7
- [ ] Genesis 29:15-30

Thursday:
- [ ] Deuteronomy 6:1-9
- [ ] Deuteronomy 22:13-29
- [ ] Exodus 21:10-11

Friday:
- [ ] Genesis 3:20-4:1
- [ ] 1 Timothy 1:12-17
- [ ] _____

FAST TRACK

Monday:
- [ ] Romans 7:1-6
- [ ] Matthew 22:23-39
- [ ] Mark 10:1-12
- [ ] _____
- [ ] _____

Tuesday:
- [ ] 1 Corinthians 13:4-7
- [ ] 1 Timothy 2:11-14
- [ ] Titus 2:3-5
- [ ] Proverb 31:10-31
- [ ] _____

Wednesday:
- [ ] 2 Corinthians 6:12-20
- [ ] Leviticus 18:6-24
- [ ] Leviticus 20:10-21
- [ ] Ephesians 6:1-9
- [ ] _____

Thursday:
- [ ] Leviticus 20:13
- [ ] Psalm 139:13-24
- [ ] Deuteronomy 24:1-4
- [ ] _____
- [ ] _____

Friday:
- [ ] 1 Corinthians 6:9-11
- [ ] Mark 3:28-30
- [ ] 2 Corinthians 2:1-8
- [ ] Romans 14:1-19
- [ ] Ecclesiastes 5:1-7

The Amplified Bible (AMP) is an English translation of the Bible produced jointly by Zondervan (subsidiary of News Corp) and The Lockman Foundation. The first edition was published in 1965, the latest in 2015. It is largely a revision of the American Standard Version of 1901, with reference made to various texts in the original languages. It is designed to "amplify" the text by using a system of punctuation and other typographical features to bring out all shades of meaning present in the original texts. Additionally, amplifications may pro-

> Matthew 19:5 And said, For this reason a man shall leave his father and mother and shall be united firmly (joined inseparably) to his wife, and the two shall become one flesh? Amplified Bible

vide further theological, historical, and other details for a better understanding of the text. Take, for example, the Greek word *pisteuo*, which is usually translated as "believe." That simple translation, however, hardly does justice to the many meanings contained in the Greek *pisteuo*: *"to adhere to, cleave to; to trust to have faith in; to rely on, to depend on."* In many ways the AMP is the classic study Bible. It combines study helps and is based on the best texts.

THIS WEEK'S QUESTION:

HEAVEN: *My Father's house has many rooms; if that were not so, would I have told you that I am going there to prepare a place for you?* - *John 14:2 NIV*

	INSIDE TRACK	MIDDLE LANES	FAST TRACK
Immortality of the Soul	**Monday:** ☐ 1 Corinthians 15:53	**Monday:** ☐ Philippians 3:7-21 ☐ 2 Timothy 1:7-12 ☐ 2 Corinthians 4:7-18	**Monday:** ☐ Matthew 19:16-30 ☐ 1 Timothy 6:12-21 ☐ Hebrews 12:6-29 ☐ 1 Peter 4:7-19 ☐ _____
The "heavens"	**Tuesday:** ☐ Genesis 1:1	**Tuesday:** ☐ Psalm 103:1-22 ☐ Luke 16:19-22 ☐ Acts 17:16-32	**Tuesday:** ☐ Matthew 3:11-17 ☐ John 3:1-27 ☐ 1 Corinthians 15:21-40 ☐ 2 Corinthians 12:1-15 ☐ Hebrews 11:1-32
"The" Heaven	**Wednesday:** ☐ John 3:12	**Wednesday:** ☐ Hebrews 1:6-14 ☐ Isaiah 65:12-17 ☐ Psalm 102:1-25	**Wednesday:** ☐ Ezekiel 1:1-26 ☐ Acts 7:42-56 ☐ 2 Peter 1:10-21 ☐ Revelation 4:1 ☐ _____
Living in Heaven	**Thursday:** ☐ Matthew 16:19	**Thursday:** ☐ Genesis 5:18-24 ☐ Matthew 6:9-33 ☐ _____	**Thursday:** ☐ 2 Kings 2:1-12 ☐ John 14:1-7 ☐ Ephesians 1:1-21 ☐ Hebrews 3:1-14 ☐ Revelation 21:1-7
What this Means to us Today	**Friday:** ☐ Ephesians 6:9	**Friday:** ☐ Romans 8:1-37 ☐ 1 Corinthians 15:45-52 ☐ Galatians 1:6-10	**Friday:** ☐ 1 Chronicles 16:1-36 ☐ Malachi 3:7-12 ☐ Matthew 5:1-12 ☐ Revelation 22:1-14 ☐ _____

The Living Oracles is a translation of the New Testament compiled and edited by Alexander Campbell (1788-1866) the early Restoration Movement leader. Published in 1826, it was based on an 1818 combined edition of translations by George Campbell, James MacKnight and Philip Doddridge, and included edits and extensive notes by Campbell. Campbell was motivated by a belief that changes in the English language and the availability of improved critical editions of the Greek New Testament had made the Authorized King James Version obsolete. The transla-

> **1 Corinthians 15:53** Wherefore, my beloved brethren, be stable, unmoved; abounding in the work of the Lord at all times, knowing that your labor is not vain in the Lord. Living Oracles

tion was widely used within the Restoration Movement, but was criticized by others for its translation of βαπτίζω (*baptizô*) as "immerse" rather than "baptize." Because of the way this word was translated, the *Living Oracles* was most often used by those who believed in immersion baptism and most vigorously criticized by groups practicing infant baptism by sprinkling. The Living Oracles was in many ways way ahead of its time. It has been called "the first modern translation." For example Phil 3.20 in the KJV reads "our conversation is in heaven"; The Living Oracles read "but we are citizens of heaven."

Growing Panes

No. 525

*H*ello,...is this Hugo McCord? I asked as I called long distance to ask my old Bible professor a serious question about a verse of Scripture. On the other end of the line, I heard that familiar southern voice say: *"That's what people have called me all my life!"* Hugo McCord, this preacher's preacher, was still translating. Nearly ninety, but still mentally sharp!

I first met brother McCord when we moved to Bartlesville, Oklahoma to begin study at what was then Central Christian College, now Oklahoma Christian University. He was the pulpit preacher at the Sixth and Dewey congregation there. He was a stately man who spoke with a southern Mississippi accent. When he was preaching God's Word, nothing took precedence...not even a crying baby! He would simply say, "Take the little one out; what I am saying here is more important than what that baby is saying!" He had a pristine respect for the Word of God.

And, his words were like beautifully strung pearls. Many of his sermons were all Scripture. Yes, that's right! *A-L-L* Bible verses memorized and strung together to form a meaningful thirty-minute sermon! At other times, his sermons were laced with pithy facts like, "when Jesus met the Samaritan woman at Jacob's well it had been giving water for 3702 years...when McCord, Gene Priest, Harold and Joe Bryant drank from the well on May 23, 1971, it took five seconds for a cup of water poured in the well to hit the water below." Or, he would go into exact detail about the *cicada, the seventeen-year locust.* He would tell how *"After mating, the female, equipped with a sharp blade, cuts under the bark of a twig, deposits her eggs, and then cuts the twigs three fourths through. As a result, the twig dies, falls to the ground, and carries the eggs to the soil. Then the eggs hatch, and the larvae dig into the ground. The adults live only about three weeks, and never see their offspring."* How? By the power of our awesome God!

McCord was a scholar. He authored more than a dozen books. His life-long dream to translate the Bible resulted in his *New Testament Translation of the Everlasting Gospel including Genesis, Psalms and Proverbs.* Regarding the value of translations to the serious Bible student, McCord wrote in the Preface to the fourth edition: "Are you married to one translation of the Bible 'until death doth us part'? Monogamy is right in marriage; but, in the area of Bible translations, a wise person will be a polygamist." The words of the prophet Habakkuk could define McCord's approach: "Write the vision and make it plain on tablets, so that a runner may read it" (2:2). E. Claude Gardener said, "The apex of his scholarly contributions is his translation...Because of his superior linguistic ability and commitment to the truth, he has prepared a translation that can be accepted with confidence by all. McCord has sought diligently to give an accurate translation of the inspired Word of God in an easily understood modern-day English."

The last time I heard brother McCord speak was at a preacher's retreat at Burnt Cabin Youth Camp in northeastern Oklahoma. He was invited to join a couple dozen preachers as the presenter for a three-day retreat. His topic was on "Preaching the Word." We all were blessed by his scholarship and personal presence. His lessons emphasized the need for preachers to keep it simple, tell the truth, and live as men of God. A memorable three days!

But, my fondest memory is this: We were camping just a couple of hundred yards from the crystal-clear Lake Ten Killer. Late one afternoon, we all decided to go to the lake for a swim. We all had brought our swimming trunks, but brother McCord had not. I can still see him walking down to that lake along with twenty-or-so preachers in his rather drab undershorts carrying a twig from a tree to swat the harassing horse flies!

Hugo McCord passed away at 8:04 a.m., May 14, 2004, in Vancouver, Washington at the home of his son Charles. Brother McCord was 92-years-old. He was a prolific writer and stalwart soldier of the cross. Truly a preacher's preacher and a talented translator of truth.

THIS WEEK'S QUESTION:

HELL: *...send Lazarus that he may dip the tip of his finger in water and cool my tongue, for I am suffering in this flame?* - *Luke 16:24 Darby Bible Translation*

WEEK 26

DATES
_____ TO _____

	INSIDE TRACK	MIDDLE LANES	FAST TRACK
The Devil and His Angels	**Monday:** ☐ Matthew 25:41	**Monday:** ☐ Revelation 12:7-9 ☐ Jude vss. 6-9 ☐ James 4:7-10	**Monday:** ☐ Genesis 3:1-7 ☐ Revelation 2:9-11 ☐ Luke 22:31-38 ☐ Matthew 4:1-11 ☐ Job 1:9-12
A Just God	**Tuesday:** ☐ Acts 10:34-35	**Tuesday:** ☐ 2 Peter 3:9 ☐ Matthew 5:44-48 ☐ 1 John 1:8-10	**Tuesday:** ☐ Romans 1:18-27 ☐ 1 Corinthians 6:9-11 ☐ Acts 2:36-47 ☐ Romans 2:4-11 ☐ _____
Hell Described	**Wednesday:** ☐ Luke 16:23-24	**Wednesday:** ☐ Revelation 14:9-12 ☐ Revelation 20:10 ☐ Revelation 21:6-8	**Wednesday:** ☐ Psalm 11:4-7 ☐ Luke 16:19-31 ☐ Luke 13:23-30 ☐ Revelation 19:11-21 ☐ _____
Hell is Real	**Thursday:** ☐ John 3:16-17	**Thursday:** ☐ James 3:6 ☐ John 3:22-36 ☐ Romans 6:23	**Thursday:** ☐ Matthew 5:21-30 ☐ Matthew 18:7-9 ☐ Mark 9:43-48 ☐ John 5:24-29 ☐ _____
What this Means to us Today	**Friday:** ☐ John 1:1-3	**Friday:** ☐ Ephesians 6:10-12 ☐ 1 Peter 5:1-11 ☐ John 12:47-50	**Friday:** ☐ Isaiah 9:1-7 ☐ Daniel 12:1-13 ☐ John 6:28-40 ☐ 2 Peter 2:4-10 ☐ 1 John 5:9-13

John 1:1-3 NTTEG
In the beginning was the Word, and the Word was with God, and the Word was God. This one was in the beginning with God. All things were created by him, and without him, nothing was created.

By diligent study, thorough academic preparation, self-discipline, and heart cultivation, Dr. Hugo McCord became one of the leading and ripest scholars in the United States. His greatest scholarly contribution was The Everlasting Gospel—New Testament with Genesis, Psalms, Proverbs and More. Because of his superior linguistic ability and commitment to the truth, he prepared a translation that can be accepted with confidence by all. He sought diligently to give an accurate translation of the inspired Word of God in an easily understood modern day English. The word 'church' is eliminated and instead McCord translates *ekklesia* as 'called out people' and 'congregation.' Instead of using 'repent', he translates the original word as 'change the heart.' McCord eliminates 'begotten' in John 3:16 and other verses, and he used 'unique.' Detailed information on these changes and others are given in the appendix. McCord (1911–2004) was an American preacher and biblical scholar within the churches of Christ in America. He taught Bible at Oklahoma Christian for many years and was a regular speaker in many churches of Christ.

Growing Panes
No. 526

Race Review Quiz

The following questions are taken from each of the twenty-six weeks of reading schedules.   This is an open book test. If you need to, go back and find the answers in the readings.

1) *In what city did Paul say we are "God's offspring"?*

A) Damascus
B) Athens
C) Rome

2) *What sin was Ananias and Sapphira guilty of committing?*

A) Stealing
B) Lying
C) Adultery

3) *Lazarus had already been dead and in the tomb for how many days when Jesus came?*

A) Two days
B) Three days
C) Four days

4) *Why had Saul gone to Carmel when Samuel came looking for him?*

A) To offer sacrifices
B) To set up a monument
C) To fight the Amalekites

5) *What did Paul tell early Christians to offer as sacrifices?*

A) Proceeds from land sold
B) A fatted calf
C) Their own bodies

6) *What is the "great" commission?*

A) God's return to us for giving
B) Go preach the Gospel
C) Become a soldier of Christ

7) *What is the church of Christ built upon?*

A) Christ as God's Son
B) Worldwide mission
C) Sacrifices of its leaders

8) *Whoever believes and _____ shall be saved.*

A) Offers the believer's prayer
B) Is baptized
C) Is a good moral person

9) *How can a person be "born again"?*

A) By being baptized
B) By Holy Spirit experience
C) By bodily reincarnation

10) *Jesus said, If you love me, you will:*

A) Fight for me
B) Keep my commandments
C) Be faithful to me

11) *Jesus' new commandment was:*

A) You love like I have loved
B) Love those who don't love you.
C). You love by being willing to die

12) *What was the church doing while Peter was in prison?*

A) Fighting among theselves
B) Planning for his release
C) Praying for his release

13) *What were the disciples arguing about on the road ?*

A) Who should prepare supper
B) How to heal a man
C) Who is the greatest

14) *What causes fights and quarrels among disciples?*

A) Differences of opinion
B) Selfish ambition
C) Too much talk

15) *If a backslider comes back, Christians should:*

A) Accept them
B) Accept on conditions
C) Accept on a trial basis

16) *Anyone who slanders a brother or sister actually:*

A) Does a good thing
B) Judges God and His law
C) Puts down evil

17) *Why is there no fear to walk in the valley of the shadow of death?*

A) My large bank account
B) My shepherd
C) My family and friends

18) *Who asked Jesus about paying tribute to Caesar?*

A) The Sadducees
B) Pharisees and Herodians
C) The Maccabees

19) *When Peter said he loved Jesus, Jesus told him to:*

A) Go preach the Gospel
B) Walk on the water
C) Feed my sheep

20) *Receiving God's forgiveness depends on this:*

A) Forgiving others
B) Giving to others
C) Saving others

21) *Who was the "firstfruits" from the dead?*

A) Elijah
B) Lazarus
C) Christ

22) *Everyone will be judged by:*

A) Laws of the land
B) Holy Spirit
C) Christ

23) *Job offered an intercessory prayer to God for forgiveness for:*

A) Himself
B) His wife
C) His three friends

24) *In a marriage, the head of the household should be the:*

A) Husband
B) Wife
C) Husband and Wife

25) *In life after death what type of bodies will we have?*

A) Mortal
B) Renewed Mortal
C) Immortal

26) *The rich man wanted father Abraham to send Lazarus to warn:*

A) His brothers
B) His best friends
C) His wife

*** READING NOTES ***

*** READING NOTES ***

www.ingramcontent.com/pod-product-compliance
Lightning Source LLC
Chambersburg PA
CBHW041221040426

42443CB00002B/33